Captain Tom Ryman

Tom Ryman family June 1903 on the front steps of their home at 514 Market Street. Front row, left to right: Pearl Ryman Coggins, Louise Ryman Buchanan, Infant Bennie (Louise) Buchanan, Tom Coggins, Tom Ryman, Elizabeth Coggins, Bettie Ryman, Lee Rol Coggins. Back row: Leslie Ryman Barton, Tom Ryman Jr., Georgia Ryman, Daisy Ryman Coggins, Paul Ryman.

Captain Tom Ryman

His Life and Legacy

Compiled and Edited by

Charmaine B. Gossett

HILLSBORO PRESS
Franklin, Tennessee

TENNESSEE HERITAGE LIBRARY

Printed in the United States of America

0 5   0 4   0 3   0 2   0 1   1   2   3   4   5

Library of Congress Catalog Card Number: 2001090280

ISBN: 1-57736-239-X

Cover design by Gary Bozeman and Elaine Kernea Wilson

Cover photos of the Ryman Auditorium by Gail Morris

HILLSBORO PRESS
PROVIDENCE HOUSE PUBLISHERS
238 Seaboard Lane • Franklin, Tennessee 37067
800-321-5692
www.providencehouse.com

Contents

List of Illustrations

SOURCES:
1   Mrs. Foster Jones Clayton and Ms. Reynolds Jones Davant
2   Tennessee State Library and Archives
3   Mrs. Thomas Proctor Jr.
4   Mrs. Gail Morris
5   Mrs. Charmaine B. Gossett
6   Metropolitan Government Archives

Preface & Acknowledgments

Through the Grand Ole Opry, the Ryman Auditorium has become known around the world and along with it so has Captain Tom Ryman, for whom the Union Gospel Tabernacle was renamed at the time of his death in 1904. Truth and myth continue to circulate about the man who at the time of his religious conversion conceived the idea of building a meeting place where large crowds could come to hear the Gospel of Jesus Christ. For those who want to know more about the man, rather than the mythical legend, this book is for you.

In putting together a genealogy for my family I found that much has been written about him, not only by his daughters, but also in the newspapers during his lifetime. As an image of the flesh and blood man developed, it occurred to me that along with his family, many would be interested in getting to know the real Tom Ryman.

This book invites you to get to know Tom Ryman as a friend. Although he achieved business success as operator of the largest steamboat line on the Cumberland River in the late 1800s, he never lost sight of his humble beginnings as a fisherman who started working with his father at age thirteen digging worms on the riverbank.

The scope of this book begins with the oral history of Tom Ryman's ancestors and concludes with the death of his children and their spouses.

Through family writings and newspaper accounts of Tom Ryman's time, the reader is invited to know him in a more down-home way. The wedding accounts are given as a way of inviting you into his home and his family circle. Tragedies are included because intimate friends share griefs as well as joys. Since this began as a genealogy, that data has been included in latter chapters of the book.

I wish to acknowledge the generous and gracious help of my late cousin Elizabeth Coggins Jones for sharing the writings of her mother,

Daisy Ryman Coggins, and her aunt, Leslie Ryman Barton. I am also grateful to Elizabeth Jones's daughter Foster Clayton of Weatherford, Texas, for providing current data on Tom Ryman's descendants and some family photographs. A special thank you goes to my Aunt Bennie (Mrs. Louise Buchanan Proctor) of Augusta, Georgia, for her love and encouragement over the years and for giving me access to her collection of family-related materials. Thanks also to Jeanne Johnson of Tarpon Springs, Florida, for her enthusiasm and contagious curiosity which lead to my completing the research I began in 1968 and to the creation of this book.

PART 1

INTRODUCTION

Meet Tom Ryman and His Family

by Charmaine B. Gossett

Let's pretend you lived years ago during the time when Tom Ryman was alive. You would have opportunity to read about him in the Nashville newspapers, hot off the press. You could read an article about raising money for the galleries in the Union Gospel Tabernacle which contains a personal letter from Tom Ryman encouraging public financial support to get the job done. You could read an account of Captain J. S. Tyner in which he tells of first working for Tom Ryman and his father, John, as a youth of fifteen and gives details of their lifelong friendship and business association as well as some of Tyner's Civil War experiences. Another newspaper account of May 18, 1902, gives a brief history of "Captain Tom Ryman's Work On the River and For Religion" which contains specific details about his religious conversion and how he acted upon the idea he conceived that night to build a Gospel Tabernacle. You would also have the opportunity to read "Last Days of Real Steamboating on the Cumberland," an excerpt from M. B. Morton's book *The Colorful Eighties in Nashville* and learn that in the 1880s the steamboat business was being replaced by the coming of the railroads, and thus better understand that Tom Ryman's career spanned the birth, pinnacle, and demise of the steamboating industry. Then, much later, after the death of Captain Ryman and his son Tom Jr., you would read about the bankruptcy of the Ryman Line.

A fact long forgotten, but which you would have been able to read about, is the shooting death of Tom Ryman Jr. who was killed as he walked up the steps to the pilot deck on the *Jo Horton Fall* steamboat. The shooter, Wilson Montgomery, was a former riverboat pilot whom Ryman Jr. had fired. After one mistrial and a second trial one year later, Montgomery was found not guilty. By reading the newspaper accounts and a summary of the court records you can come to your own conclusion about how that verdict came about.

Let's pretend even further that you have an opportunity to personally listen to some of his family members as they tell you about their father and their early childhood. This book contains all the writings of his daughters Daisy and Leslie on the milestones in their parent's lives, such as how their parents met. It also contains a description of Tom and Bettie's honeymoon trip aboard Tom's first steamboat, *Alpha,* with thirty-five of their friends as told by the bride's sister. The family writings also include a personal account of Tom Ryman's incarceration by the Union Army during the Civil War, as well as his wife's eyewitness account of her experience as a young girl during the Battle of Franklin.

When Tom and Bettie first married, their home was on the *Alpha* as it steamed up and down the Cumberland and Ohio rivers transporting freight and passengers. The Ryman children accompanied their parents. These writings will also reveal an indulgent father who let them blow the steamboat whistle for a landing and visit in the pilothouse around coffee time.

You could also read newspaper articles about Tom Ryman's death and his funeral which was attended by four thousand people in the Union Gospel Tabernacle. The articles tell how the name of the tabernacle was changed to Ryman Auditorium, something that Tom Ryman had refused to permit during his lifetime. Some of these articles read like a brief biography of Tom Ryman and can give the reader a further insight into the character of the man.

As time passes, you would read about the death of a daughter, then the death of his wife, the death of another daughter, a son-in-law, and so on, until all members of the immediate family and their spouses are gone, bringing a closure to this family circle.

Why is Tom Ryman still remembered? Not for his steamboat empire; that era has come and gone, but for what he did for Christ, the building of a tabernacle where all denominations could come together to hear the Gospel preached.

"Follow me, and I will make you fishers of men," said Jesus in Matthew 4:19. On the granite monument centered on the Ryman lot at Mount Olivet Cemetery there are two carvings. On the west side is a steamboat with the name "T. G. Ryman" on the paddle wheel. On the east side is a fishing boat and net, depicting not only his early life as a fisherman, but symbolizing his obedience to Christ to be a fisher of men. We find out in Daisy's chapter "A Benediction" that in addition to having originated the idea of the Gospel Tabernacle and worked diligently for its funding, he also instigated and funded other Christian works. Tom Ryman is an example of what God can do with a man who whole-heartedly gives his life to Jesus Christ.

When the Grand Ole Opry was broadcast from the Ryman Auditorium, there was a continuation of the purpose for which the taber-nacle was built and dedicated because the majority of the country music performers included hymns and gospel songs in their segments of the program. In this way, each Saturday night the Gospel was not only proclaimed to those seated in the auditorium, but to thousands listening over the airwaves.

Tom Ryman would have enjoyed these performances, not only for the religious emphasis, but the upbeat mountain music and down-home humor. He was not a long-faced, somber Christian, but one that enjoyed life and the company of other people having a good time. I hope you will enjoy meeting him and his family in the pages of this book.

Dispelling an Erroneous Myth

by Charmaine B. Gossett

Legends die hard, and it seems for Tom Ryman an erroneous legend revives periodically. Herein, attempt will be made to put forth the true facts and set the record straight about his conversion and the tale of his pouring barrels of whiskey from his bars into the Cumberland River.

To know the truth is to know Tom Ryman the man, and not the myth.

The most current published account of the myth at the time of this writing occurred in 1996 and says:[1]

The year was 1885. Horses and buggies rattled over the cobblestones of downtown Nashville as a huge crowd gathered beneath a sprawling tent. The draw is Sam Jones, a Georgia preacher famous for his fire-and-brimstone brand of evangelism.

Just down the road from there, the riverfront played host to a different breed of folks. The rowdies and roustabouts who hung around there frequently had their fun by barging in on these revivals and heckling the preacher. Riverboat captain Tom Ryman was sometimes among the instigators.

But legend has it that on this particular evening, as Ryman and his buddies were beginning their usual mischief, Ryman began to listen to Jones' sermon. As he listened, he realized that Jones was talking about something as sacred to the captain as the river itself: mother.

Thereafter, Tom Ryman became one of Jones' most ardent converts. . . . and legend has it that Ryman went directly back to his saloon and began

5

pouring barrels of whiskey into the Cumberland River, ordering all of his steamboats up and down the river to do the same.

It's a colorful story, and sells tickets, but the tale is just what Gaylord Entertainment Company says it is, a legend.

The origin of the legend is unknown. The earliest recorded account of the story and it being refuted can be found in the December 24, 1904, *Nashville Banner* article about Tom Ryman's funeral. "After Capt. Ryman had been converted the leases for the bar privileges on his various boats were taken up as they expired, and he has not permitted one to be run on one of his boats since. An idea has become prevalent that he poured many barrels of whiskey into the river at this time, but this story is without foundation."

M. B. Morton, in "Last Days of Real Steamboating on the Cumberland," which appeared in the *Nashville Banner*, also refutes the myth. "It has been said that after his conversion he destroyed all the bars on his steamboats. They were leased to the men who conducted them. He did, however, notify these men that he would lease no more bar room privileges; and in this way the Ryman Line became dry."[2]

The legend was further perpetuated by the widow of Sam Jones and her coauthor Rev. Walter Holcomb. Their book *Life and Sayings of Sam P. Jones* published in 1907 records the conversion experience of Tom Ryman as: "He was an old steamboat captain, who owned a number of steamboats which plied the Cumberland River, and considerable property along the wharf, and in one of his large buildings he had a large saloon. He had a bar on each of his steamboats. . . . He was brought to Christ by the preaching of Mr. Jones, and became a Christian in dead earnest. He cleaned out the bars on his steamers, tossed his liquors overboard. His saloon was converted into a hall for religious and temperance meetings . . ."[3]

Mrs. Jones further says "At the memorial service held in the auditorium in memory of Mr. Jones, a rising vote of the thousands packed into the building, changed its name to 'The Jones-Ryman Auditorium' in honor of Mr. Jones, who inspired it, and the other who executed the plan."[4] The inaccuracy of this statement is evident today.

The Ryman and Jones families became close friends. The zealousness of a devoted wife and coworker who perpetuated the erroneous legend as they recorded the accomplishments of a man whom they dearly loved and who was truly one of the greatest evangelists of his time, can easily be forgiven. No malice was intended. It just made a good story better.

The legend again resurfaced in 1948 in an article in the *Nashville Banner*, and was quickly refuted by an acquaintance of Captain Ryman in a letter to the editor. Paul W. Treanor wrote:

> In your article on the visit of Dr. Walt Holcomb of Atlanta and the time Capt. Tom Ryman was converted by Sam Jones. . . . It is said that he dumped his whiskey in the river, [and] closed his big saloon. . . . Now, at the time Captain Ryman was converted by Sam Jones he did not close any "big saloon" as he did not have any saloons to close. He did not even operate the bar on his steamboat but that was a concession that was leased to two river men, Alex Longinette and George Jobes. . . . I write this that the record be kept straight about Capt. Ryman on the whiskey question. He was not buying or selling liquor. He was not on either side of the bar.[5]

Maybe the legend originated by a reporter with an active imagination, who visualized Tom Ryman as a colorful Mark Twain–type river character. True he had a gregarious, flamboyant personality and a philosophy that "amusements are necessary in order to give a completeness to life."[6] Although fun loving, he was not irreverent to religion, disrespectful or condescending to rich or poor. As a young lad Tom was strongly influenced by his mother and grandmother Amy Green who was a deeply religious woman, very active in her church. In fact, upon his conversion, he joined the Elm Street Methodist Church, of which his Grandmother Green had been a charter member.

With so many witnesses, hopefully, this settles the myth of Captain Ryman's pouring the whiskey into the river. But there still remains another part of the conversion story that is also a myth, Capt. Ryman and his rowdy crew going to the meeting with the intent of heckling the preacher.

Sam Jones preached in various Nashville churches in February of 1885 and was invited to return in May for a three-week tent revival. It was a major event for the people of Nashville to be able to hear one of the greatest evangelists of their day and the whole city was eagerly anticipating Mr. Jones's return. Throngs of people turned out for the meetings. So many that the tent was not able to hold them all and many choose to remain on the outside of the tent to hear the great preacher.

In May of 1885 Tom Ryman was forty-three years old and in the process of building his house at 514 Market Street (now Second Avenue South). The only rowdy crew he took with him to the meeting were his wife and six children, ranging from age four to fifteen years. And they were interested enough to get there in time to be seated in the tent because he tells of seeking out his friends after his conversion and finding them outside the tent. His purpose was to tell them about his conversion experience and encourage them to also make a profession of faith in Jesus Christ as Savior and Lord if they had not done so already.[7]

It was at this meeting that Tom Ryman saw the need for a larger meeting place so that all Christian denominations could come together under one roof to hear the Gospel preached and he lost no time in sharing this idea with Sam Jones and many of his friends and business associates. But that is another story, the details of which can be read in the newspaper accounts found in chapters 17, 18, and 19 of this book.

PART 2

FAMILY
WRITINGS

from Daisy's Book, *by Daisy Coggins, date unknown*

Early Life of My Father

by Daisy Ryman Coggins

My father had very little formal schooling. In his teens his father died and it was up to him to support a large family: his mother, three sisters and one younger brother.

His father, a comparatively young man, died leaving this responsibility on his shoulders. His father left a thriving business and a moderate estate. He was a fisherman and owned a fleet of fishing boats on the Cumberland River which operated out of Nashville in camps along the river. These were early times when the Cumberland River was filled with fish, and it was a profitable business.

My father grew up in camps along the river. He was as much at home in the water as he was on the land. He developed a robust physique with all this outdoor exercise. He learned to handle boats and to do all the heavy physical work preparing fish for market.

The boats, of course, were larger than skiffs, but were operated by hand and the fish were caught by seines and trotlines.

My father, although so young when his father died, took over the business and operated it quite successfully. He employed numbers of men, some of whom were half owners, and his equal in intelligence and ability. One of these, Mr. Tyner, stayed with my father after he developed his own line of steamboats operating to Evansville, Indiana, out of Nashville to the Upper Cumberland.

At that time the river was the main artery of travel also for shipping freight of all kinds. If anyone wanted to travel to Nashville, they could come over on horseback and, of course, if they had freight to ship they could build a raft of logs, which were easy to obtain, and float to Nashville.

This was a business in itself, because several neighbors would work together and build a raft by binding logs together on the underside and build a shelter in the center. Then they would simply put a thick mud floor on the space where they expected to work in the day-time and night-time. They made it thick enough to cook on so the logs would not catch fire when they cooked.

Of course, they could travel downstream only, and this was dangerous because of the current, the sandbars, and the rocks, and they had to know the stream. The only guide they had was the judgment of the man in charge. Whoever acted as pilot had to know something of the current, sandbars, and rocks. The rocks especially were what they had to avoid. A bad collision with the rocks would tie up the boat. But they were hardy men and did not mind that.

If they were from the mountains and had goods to sell in Nashville, the wharf in Nashville was a busy place. It was in easy reach of the wholesale merchants who would buy anything they had to sell—from chickens, meat, cotton, field crops, to moonshine—more of that than anything else. There was plenty of that made and sold. If Nashville was as far as they were going, they sold their rafts in Nashville to sawmills immediately adjacent to the wharf.

They had a glorious time doing the town, and as the town had plenty of saloons they got plenty drunk. They bought a horse and rode home if they could; if they had not spent so much of their money on liquor.

By this time my father had made enough money in the fishing business to buy a small boat which would carry both passengers and freight. His return trips up the Cumberland periodically carried many of these raftsmen home to the mountains.

One experience my father had during the Civil War; he was arrested and imprisoned by the Yankees. I have no idea what charges were brought against him, but in prison his characteristic industry proved profitable to him. The camp was not supplied with water, it was necessary to carry the water to the prisoners from the spring. My father carried water to the prisoners and charged them for doing it.[1]

In the course of some days, he was released, probably through the efforts of his mother and members of the firm. He was personally pardoned by Andrew Johnson. In gratitude for the Governor's clemency, he cleaned and prepared the best fish he could find, and proceeded to the Governor's mansion to deliver it. He did not expect to see the Governor, but he did and the Governor was very pleased and gracious.[2]

[Another account of the Civil War imprisonment recorded by Mrs. T. W. Bookhart as related to her by Tom Ryman circa 1903 is given below.][3]

During the War between the States, Mr. Ryman was engaged in the river business for the Confederacy. He used seven fishing boats and forty men. He related the following incident:

One day I received an order supposed to have been sent by the government. It commanded me to go up the river some three miles above Jacksonville, Tennessee, and land at the mouth of the creek at twelve o'clock at night. This seemed a very unusual hour, and my mother and sisters began to insist that I should not go as they suspected some foul play. I got in a boat and towed well up the river, keeping well in the middle of the stream. I placed my gun in the bottom of the boat and kept my pistol in my pocket, ready for an emergency.

When I was opposite the mouth of the creek I gave a big shove with my oar, making toward the land. At the same time I seized my gun with one hand and my pistol in the other and stepped out on land.

A call came, "Halt." The voice was that of a Union officer who stood on the bank with some of his men.

I said, "I'll shoot to kill if you do not make your men lay down their arms until we have a word."

This was done and trouble was averted. The officer told me that Jeff Woodward, an orphan boy whom my parents had reared, had reported that I was carrying arms to the enemy. I had no way at that time to prove my innocence. It was one man's word against another's. I was therefore arrested and carried to Paducah, Kentucky, and put in prison. Every time water was wanted I would volunteer to go for it. One day I found a man who said he would help me to escape.[4] I had written to my people about my plight and begged that they would come and bring proof of my innocence. Before Mother could reach Kentucky the man of whom I have spoken helped me make an escape. I came back by rail to Nashville while Mother was en route to Paducah by boat.

Jeff Woodward made his way to Wisconsin, and after so long a time I received a letter from him confessing his guilt, and asking for my forgiveness.

This was a most terrible ordeal.

The fall of Fort Donelson down the river at Dover led to the capture of Nashville and the downfall of the Confederacy. My father's management of his business during the Civil War when the Cumberland River played an important part resulted in profits to his family and all concerned.

By this time the river business was developed. The big Mississippi steamers could navigate the Cumberland to Nashville in high water. During the winter this was dangerous traveling for the boats, especially as they could make it only when the river was high.

This season lasted only for the winter months and there was considerable travel by steamboat. But the necessity for travel was always increasing and as the steamboat business was increasing the social life in Nashville was increasing.

Therefore, my father's ambitions increased and turned to dreams of a packet line all his own, which would be boats for carrying passengers and freight. To this end, he saved his money, his personal share of the profits of the business, until he had accumulated $3,000, which he estimated would be the cost of a steamboat with which he could begin to carry out his object of having a packet line of his own on the Cumberland. Armed with the cash in bills, his mother dressed him for a raft trip down to New Orleans. She sewed the money into the lining of his coat, and he joined the other passengers on such a raft as I have described earlier.

Of course, he could not take off his coat when he went to bed in such a crude accommodation that the brush arbor furnished. But, as he traveled south it got hotter and hotter and he perspired freely but he could not take off his coat. He was afraid to.

He reached New Orleans, found the boat he wanted, and bought her. He prepared for his trip up the Mississippi. He hired a pilot and laid up his boat. He had no knowledge of the Mississippi River, and he was depending on his pilot for that, but after some disagreements between them, in his usual impulsive way, he fired the pilot and determined to take his boat home alone. After an arduous time, he arrived at Nashville with his first boat, which appropriately enough was named *Alpha*, the first letter of the Greek alphabet. This was the first step toward his own packet line.

The *Alpha* paid for herself in a few years. She was a very crude little boat but she made money until he was able to build the *Eddyville*, which was named for a town on the Cumberland River. The ladies of Eddyville presented the boat with a very handsome silver water service. The tray has an inscription and what is left of this water service is still in the family. She was a very pretty boat with a very pretty cabin.

Then the captain of this boat was married, and his bride left with him on the boat, and she became the official hostess to the passengers, as the captain's wife always is.

The marriage ceremony took place in Franklin, Tennessee, my mother's home. The wedding party, which consisted of thirty-five guests, was entertained on this boat with a week's trip to Eddyville and Evansville and return. There was an orchestra to furnish music for dancing and there were all kinds of fun and frolic for the entire week.

My mother lived with her family in Nashville at such intervals as she left the boat. My mother said of course it was a new life for her, but she enjoyed it.

My father said she was a fine hostess and helper. She helped him to build up his business. Her great good sense and sincere interest in the passengers gave her an intelligent concept of how she could help him. She made many friends, friends for a lifetime.

She said like all brides she had homesick moments. One of these was when the boat passed the Harpeth River. She said she always shed a few tears when the boat passed the mouth of the Harpeth. Her home town, Franklin, Tennessee, was on this small river.

from Daisy Ryman Coggins's collection of family papers, circa 1903–1926

Reminiscences of Mama's Childhood
(Mary Elizabeth "Bettie" Baugh Ryman)

by Leslie Ryman Barton and Mrs. T. W. Bookhart

Wyatt Woodruff Baugh married Sarah Elizabeth Neely, and to them was born three children. The eldest, a daughter called Mary Elizabeth "Bettie," was born January 3, 1847, some twelve miles south of Franklin, Tennessee.

The Baugh home at that time was very unpretentious, being a one-room log cabin. The windows were overhung with homespun, and home-made shades, and the children of the family always peeped under instead of drawing them aside for fear of making wrinkles or causing a rent.

Her mother [Sarah] liked to tell the story of when they were first married she decided to make a suit for her husband. She carded, spun and wove cloth, then cut it out, basted and fitted it. It was all sewed by hand and needle and after it was finished she had Wyatt try it on. He replied that it was okay. Upon closer examination Sarah found that she had sewed the left sleeve in the right armhole and vice versa, but neither one said a word. Thereupon she ripped it out and fixed it. Afterwards Wyatt did confess he knew it didn't feel exactly right.

When Bettie was five years old, she and her sister, Alabama, known as Sis Tom, who was only three, used to stand and watch for Captain Kidd, who drove the stagecoach drawn by six horses, as he journeyed from Nashville to Columbia, Tennessee. At the sound of a blast from his elk horn, the children would run and wave their hands at their friend. Wyatt Baugh carried the mail to and from the train and Captain Kidd would pick it up at their house.

Bettie remembered riding on the first train which went into Nashville in company with her father and little sister, Sis Tom, and a friend whose name was Mr. Littleton, a shoe merchant of Franklin, Tennessee. Before there was a positive promise that Bettie and Sis Tom could go, their mother told them that they must cut and tack ten balls, which were as big as your head, for a rag carpet. Her mother always kept a rag carpet making, usually completing one per year. To make ten balls before time for the trip seemed almost an impossibility to their childish minds, but they determined to go at any cost. Therefore, they worked honestly until the last night before they were to go, then they resorted to using strategy. Rolling up rags as a foundation, they began cutting and winding the tacked strips until each ball gained the proper proportions. In due time ten large carpet balls were placed in their mother's work basket ready for the weaving of the rag carpet. Afterwards they took out the wadded centers and fixed them right without their mother knowing what they had done.

Mama's father was an overseer for a Mr. Carter and received $100.00 a year. Fifty dollars went to pay on a lot in Franklin. After it was paid for, he built a house. After the family moved to Franklin, Wyatt Baugh wanted to buy some corn from Mr. Carter and asked about it. Carter said he had none to sell. "Well, I'll buy it from Jack" (a Negro Carter owned). So the Negro sold Carter corn to Wyatt and was paid money for the corn.

Mama and Sis Tom as wee children used to steal sugar out of an old sugar chest which was so tall they had to balance themselves on the edge of the bin when sugar was low in the chest. One day they heard their mother coming so Mama and Sis Tom ran and crawled under the house, Mama first, but before Sis Tom could get under there their mother caught her by the feet and she got her punishment. Mama had to come out and get hers. They each had hands full of sugar and divided [them] after the spankings.

Mama was twelve years old when her father died in Franklin, Tennessee, and he is buried there in Hope Cemetery.

from Daisy Ryman Coggins's collection of Ryman family papers

Reminiscences of the Battle of Franklin

by Mrs. T. W. Bookhart and Mary Elizabeth "Bettie" Baugh Ryman

Bettie was about thirteen years old when the War between the States was declared. She helped her mother make eighty-eight caps for the First Regiment to leave Franklin, Tennessee. Afterwards, on several occasions, Bettie carried articles of clothing through the lines to the Confederate soldiers. Bettie saw much of the suffering caused by the cruel war and related many things of great interest to me concerning these trying days.

She was an eyewitness to part of Hood's disastrous campaign around Franklin. Below is her personal account of the events.

Mother and I had been watching from our house all day and in the afternoon decided to go to Uncle Wesley Neely's to see what was going on. Uncle Wesley had a storm cellar and we thought we would be safe there in case of an immediate danger. The next day we returned home. I had to go to McGavock's store on an errand and while there the Yankee army fell back. When I got back home Mother, Sis Tommie, my brother Dea, and I were first upstairs and then down. We were very much disturbed as we watched the Federal soldiers turning their horses into our yard. We had little food in the house which consisted of about two pounds of flour, a pound of cornmeal, and two small pieces of dried beef.

A neighbor, Mr. Moss, came over and told Mother that his wife was very sick, and begged that she would give her aid. Mother always ready, went to the Moss' home and found Mrs. Moss was frightened nearly to death. Of course we went with Mother and Mother begged us to run and hide in Uncle Wesley's cellar, but Sis Tommie refused to go. Mother promised to come to us but she did not get there as the Battle of Franklin began.

A number of people spent the night in Mr. and Mrs. Moss' woodshed. A neighbor ran in and told them that as she was coming, she saw a Yankee shot down on the street. The next day Mother and I went back home and Confederates had found six Yankees asleep in our beds. They had not bothered to remove their boots which were covered with mud. Mother was asked if she wanted to search them to see whether they had robbed her or not. Mother told them that she would not care to search them. They had cooked all the food which we had except the bran from the meal. With this Mother made a hoecake for breakfast. The neighbors, hearing of our plight, sent in some food and that day for dinner we served sixteen Confederate soldiers a meal of pork and beans.

Many dead Yankees were on the street. A Negro man came in during the day, and brought a wounded soldier who was too ill to move on to the hospital, and Mother took him in to nurse. They proved to be James Brandon from Mississippi and his body servant. Later in the day, Captain Burgess was brought in very badly wounded. We did all we could for them. Mr. Brandon after four months of suffering was sent to prison at Columbus, Ohio, in an army wagon. A Mr. Fox wrote Mother that Mr. Brandon was not doing well, and that if something was not done for him he would die. Mr. Fox asked Mother to go to Ohio to see what she could do about getting him paroled. Mother and Mr. Brandon's brother-in-law went together and after much red tape, they got him paroled. They took him to Louisville, Kentucky, and then he took a boat for Mississippi.

When Mr. Brandon was in Franklin, Ned, his body-servant, would go out and buy things for his master to eat. When Mr. Brandon was wounded he gave his horse to General Claybourne [*sic*]. General Claybourne was afterwards killed and his horse received 32 bullet holes in her.[1]

During the Battle of Franklin [November 30, 1864], Uncle Marion Neely stopped at Uncle Wesley's to speak to the family. He was in Company C, Forrest Cavalry. He found them in the cellar. He said, "I'm disgusted about all this talk of soldiers being starved to death. We yet have parched corn."

Later several Federal soldiers ran in and tried to take refuge in the cellar, and Uncle Wesley made them leave. This was a terrible time. Shells were falling everywhere, and the dead were scattered as far as could be seen.

During the siege around Franklin I went to stay with Aunt Sallie Arms for a few days. Aunt Sallie's husband was in the army. They had such a fine full-blooded horse, and we lived in terror of it being taken. When the Federals came there they found a yard full of chickens. The cavalrymen cut the fowls down with their swords, and Aunt Sallie and I would run and get them and throw them as far as we could under the house. All of the chickens were slaughtered except one cock. Aunt Sallie was cooking a pot of pigfeet when the Federals came and they ran their hands in the pot and took the meat out. They stole the sausage meat from the table. They destroyed all of her meat and took everything from the pantry. They took her cow and tried to twist her tail and head together and milked her dry.

Mother and her family, together with their neighbors, had taken refuge in Uncle Wesley's cellar. The Federal troops had captured the fort across the Harpeth River section, nearest Nashville, when the Confederates came into Franklin. The Federals would go back and forth and shell the town. It was therefore very dangerous to be seen on the road or street.

During a lull, Mother ran upstairs to get a view of what was going on. Not being able to see well from all the windows there she hastened up into the attic which had two windows. There was a bed pulled across the window on the side nearest the Presbyterian church. Mother, being tired, laid down on the bed, and rolled a quilt up and placed it under her head for a pillow. When she looked out, she saw the Confederates coming, whereupon she ran downstairs calling, "They come! They come!" Some ran to the corner to see them coming. Just as Mother left her bed, a shell burst and came through the window where she had lately been resting and drove a portion of the quilt through the wall. If she had stayed a few minutes longer, she would have been blown to pieces.

The Confederates proved to be Forrest's Cavalry.

Mother took all of us to the McGavock farm for safety. They began to bring in the wounded. Mrs. McGavock had a new bolt of domestic, which she gladly used for bandages. After this was exhausted, they used all of the bed linen. By and by the beds were full of wounded, and the floors and even in the yard. I waited on the wounded all night. A campfire was built at the feet of each wounded soldier for warmth. So many terrible things happened that I could write volumes on the subject.

Mama's Schooling and
How She Met My Father

by Leslie Ryman Barton

My mother was educated at an Episcopal school in Franklin, Tennessee. The Episcopal rector was principal of the school and besides the regular studies of grammar school, the girls were taught embroidery, art, and sewing. The atmosphere of the place was very genteel.

My mother's only sister said that mother's behavior was always perfect. She [Mother] was a good student and had a lovely disposition, but she, Sis Tom, was of the opposite temperament. Not only did she do her own fighting on the recess grounds, but my mother's as well. This opinion is collaborated by a beautiful little prayer book which was given to my mother for excellent scholarship and behavior. I still have the book. The inscription in the front reads: "Mary E. Baugh, A token of respect and esteem from her sincere friend. S/George N. James, Franklin, Tenn., 11th November 1859." In Bettie's handwriting is the verse: "The wise took oil in their vessels with their lamps. Matt. 25:4."

My mother wrote an exquisite Italic hand which she learned at school and all her life she did beautiful handwork of all kinds, although she said she was so busy with practical things after she married that she had very little time for embroidery, sewing, crocheting, etc.

Her education was continued at Franklin College near Nashville, a school founded by Tolbert Fanning and his brother Jack. These men were English and highly cultured. Tolbert was a wonderful orator and a preacher in the Christian Church. He edited a magazine, and was a powerful factor in the pioneer founding of the Christian Church in Nashville.

The schedule was rather Spartan; it began at daylight. The assembly hall was held near the ringing of the bell and classes began near sunrise.

There was one piano only, which was in the assembly hall, and my mother and her roommate Susan Ryman had their practice hours begin at daylight and they kept each other company at that early hour, which was the only available time for them to practice.

This was a coed school. The girls' dormitory was some distance from the boys' dormitory and there was a deadline which could not be crossed from either side, but one of the alumni, who became a famous preacher, said there was nothing to prevent kisses from being thrown across the way.

Once when there was a fire all rules were suspended and students enjoyed it and mingled together sociably and enjoyed breaking hickory nuts.

This roommate, Susan, lived in Nashville and my mother was invited to spend a weekend with the family. My father-to-be was sent to drive out to the school to take them into the city to Susan's home, and he said on his part it was love at first sight, because she [Mother] was not only pretty, but she was so shy that she could not talk to him. And strange to say he seemed to like it because she was so backward.

This was the beginning of her acquaintance with my father and it culminated in her marriage to him several years later.

A Reconstruction Wedding

by Mrs. Alabama Rountree

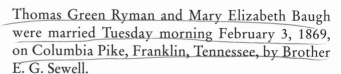

Thomas Green Ryman and Mary Elizabeth Baugh were married Tuesday morning February 3, 1869, on Columbia Pike, Franklin, Tennessee, by Brother E. G. Sewell.

The bride's maids were Susie Ryman and Alabama Baugh Rountree, called "Sis Tom."[1] The groom's men were Captain William Gracey and William Crutcher. The guests on the bridal trip to Evansville were Misses Louisa Black and Mary Black, Miss Maggie Weaver and Mrs. Mansfield from Nashville, Tennessee, and Johnny McPhail, Newman Denman, Captain Mat Gracey and Hop Johnson of Clarksville, and Mrs. Wood, Miss Mariah Gracey, Mrs. Childress and the two Miss Childress of Eddyville.

The bride's dress was of blue empress cloth trimmed in white silk alpaca with a long train. She, having had typhoid fever the summer previous, had her hair cut short and wore it in curls all over her head. Susie's dress and mine were lavender grey with train trimmed in black silk ruffles, three deep, pinked on the edge, or picoted as we would say now. The men were dressed in Prince Albert broadcloth.

The marriage took place at 8 a.m. and we left on the 9:00 a.m. train for Nashville. Louisa Black, who was visiting Franklin and one of the invited guests on the trip to Evansville, went with us to Nashville. Only a few relatives and friends witnessed the ceremony.

Arriving at Nashville about 10:00 a.m. we drove to the Ryman residence at 227 College Street where the bride was introduced to Mrs. Ryman, his mother, and his two sisters, Mrs. Molly Mansfield and Emma, the latter a school girl, then all the rest of the party were introduced. A short stay, and we all drove to the boat. Mrs. Mansfield accompanied us. Arriving there, we were joined by the rest of the guests for the trip, this being our first trip on the *Alpha*, the first boat Tom owned. He was the captain, William Gracey head clerk, and Wallace McBride, second clerk. A string band furnished the music for the trip and dancing was a great feature of the trip.

At Clarksville next morning we were joined by the party from there, and later by the Eddyville party when we reached there. By the time we reached Evansville all had become acquainted and were having a famous good time. Mr. McBride had the air "I would like to," but did not have the courage to join in the activities. Captain Gracey proposed that the girls go in a body to the office, backed up by the young men, and invite him out to join the fun. He was so evidently embarrassed when we went down and so timid after our insisting on his dancing, that we left after his promise not that night, but the next, if we would let him off. Tom enjoyed this very much.

Captain Gracey said next morning he was sure he would keep his promise because he had caught him behind one of the smoke stacks shuffling his feet trying to learn how to dance. He did keep his promise, and was so delighted with his experience that Tom said he could hardly keep him in the office long enough to attend to business. We had a rare week of pleasure. Everything was done for our comfort and pleasure. We danced in the morning, afternoon, and night.

After going ashore at the most important places, visiting Cumberland Iron Works and the Hillman Works, we played Fox-in-the-Morning and Base when ashore. Arriving in Evansville we took in the city, had our pictures taken in small groups as the party had drawn apart by mutual congenialities on the principle of "birds of a feather flock together." I don't remember whether sister had her picture taken in her bridal dress on this trip or later.

After leaving Evansville, we landed at Shawnee Town, went up in an elevator and all were weighed. Sister weighed 117 pounds. I don't remember the weight of any of the others. Arriving back in the Cumberland River, we encountered a rival boat, the *Tyrone*, and the race was on, as always was the case. The passengers and crew on each boat were soon aroused to the highest pitch of enthusiastic rivalry and partnership; the gibes and shouts passing to and fro in the boasting manner. Once the boats touched each other and one of the roustabouts jumped aboard the *Tyrone*, grabbed a rival roister and dragged him aboard the *Alpha*. He soon got himself loosened and made a spring and regained the *Tyrone*. The excitement grew more intense as the *Tyrone* gained on us, and finally passed, and the passengers waved their handkerchiefs in farewell. The roustabouts threw ropes to take us in tow and the gibes and guys were something fierce. Tom could not stand it; he rushed below, said something to the fireman and engineer, and the thing was done. Soon we were speeding along, gaining at each stroke. Once more the excitement became intense, but we surged ahead, and as we passed with shouts and jeers with band playing, we waved our handkerchiefs in farewell and one of our party wept into his handkerchief as though the parting was forever. Johnny McPhail ran and got the water cooler, rested it on the rail of the guard, waved his hand for them to be still while he took their picture, and Mr. Denman grabbed a table cloth and threw it over him—the roisters shouting, dancing and guying them. "See you later." "Catch on behind." "See you in Nashville," etc. We sailed away very proud of the victory, and the *Tyrone* seeing herself defeated, soon landed to cover her chagrin.

The last night aboard we all agreed to get up before breakfast and have a dance put forward, which we did and which closed our very enjoyable trip, for as soon as breakfast was over, the whistle blew for Nashville; then the party broke up never again to meet as a whole.

from Daisy's Book *by Daisy Ryman Coggins, date unknown*

Papa's First Boat, the *Alpha*

by Leslie Ryman Barton as told by "Bettie" Baugh Ryman

In 1867 Thomas Green Ryman rafted to New Orleans to buy a boat; the money was sewed in his coat by his mother and he remarked afterwards, "I liked to have smothered to death." He dared not take the coat off and the weather grew hotter as he traveled southward. The sum of $3,000 which nearly smothered him was transferred to Owen Davis & Brothers for the steamer *Alpha*, which had been laid up at New Orleans for the duration of the Civil War.

The unavoidable hand of fate stretched forth, for as the boat started out the wheel broke apart in the river. His uncle, Captain Charles Ryman, brought the boat home as Tom Ryman did not have his Master's license at that time. Fate grasped further and we find the steamer was cast upon a rock at Harpeth Shoals on one of her few trips in low water. As Tom was only a fisherman he had asked his Uncle Charlie Ryman to take charge of her, which he did. However, Charlie Ryman's first attempt to free the boat from rocks was unsuccessful, so Tom offered a suggestion to his uncle of a different way to do it. Their discussion heated up. His uncle said, "Why don't you do it yourself?" Tom replied, "Go to the office and get your money." So as an amateur he freed the boat in half an hour himself.

The *Alpha* ran from Paducah, Kentucky, up the Cumberland River to Nashville as long as low water would permit, then up to Clarksville, then to Dover Shoals. Steamer *Alpha* was run two years before Papa and Mama were married, then two years after, before building of the steamer *Eddyville*.

The *Alpha* competed against six other steamers running from Nashville to Clarksville and as the river fell from Clarksville to Dover

Three Ryman Line packets at the Nashville Wharf (c. 1900). Left to right: J. B. Richardson, Bob Dudley, *and* H. W. Buttorff.

Shoals at which place the amateur captain had taken charge of the boat and discharged his uncle.

During one trip from Clarksville to Evansville in low water, the shaft broke. His rivals laughed and said, "Surely we have you now." But Tom clamped the shaft to the wheel and steered to Paducah. There he repaired the boat. Afterwards he built the *Eddyville* at Evansville. While there they stayed at Ed Murry's house across Pigeon Creek. Ed Murry built Tom Ryman's steamboat called *Eddyville.* Mama and Daisy saw the *Eddyville* launched at Evansville. The *Eddyville* was begun on a Friday, launched on a Friday, and began her first trip on Friday. Her maiden trip began January 21, 1872.

Papa sold the *Alpha*'s hull for $500 and the boilers for $500 to Conauth's Mill in Smithland, Kentucky. He was going to use the texas of the *Alpha* on the new boat, but an old friend, Banwell, persuaded him not to use the old cabin. Papa borrowed $2,000 from John Sinzich (a boat store man), insured the boat for $3,000 and gave the policy as security to John Sinzich. He borrowed $500 from Ben Egan and paid 25% for use of the money. He sold privileges of the bar on the boat to

John H. Crouch for $500 at Dycusburg, Kentucky.

Another incident about the adventures of the *Alpha* occurred in 1874. It was February and the *Alpha* was on the Ohio River. There was a gorge at Caseyville that caught five other boats. The *Alpha* was in the lot. Bets were made in Nashville that if a boat was saved it would be Tom Ryman's boat. Papa placed jugs under the ice equipped with powder and fuse and blew up the ice and Papa went to bat with his boat.

On another trip while going up river the *Alpha* ran a tree up into the hull through the deck. Tom sawed off the tree inside the hull even with the bottom of the boat, took ham skin and put it on the tree from the inside of the hull and backed the boat off.

Papa always secured iron for boilers from Hillman Iron Works which guaranteed them never to blow up and filled the guarantee.

Below is a list of boats owned or co-owned by Papa. The starred boats were built by him.

1. *Alpha*
2. *Eddyville,** built at Evansville, Indiana
3. *Shipper's Own,** built at Brownsville, Pennsylvania in 1873
4. *B. S. Rhea,** built at Jeffersonville, Indiana
5. *Alex Perry,** built Jeffersonville, Indiana, 1891
6. *J. P. Droulliard*, Jeffersonville, Indiana
7. *I. T. Rhea*, Jeffersonville, Indiana (This boat sank thirteen times and always on the 13th of the month. The last time she sank in the Upper Cumberland Captain Ryman refused to raise her, "Let her machinery lay and rust in the water.")
8. *Ashland City*, built Jeffersonville, Indiana, 1892
9. *W. K. Phillips,** built Jeffersonville, Indiana, 1892
10. *H. W. Buttorff**
11. *J. B. Richardson,** last boat he built, Jeffersonville, Indiana, 1898
12. *Bob Dudley,** running to Celina and Burnside
13. *Reuben Dunbar,** built Jeffersonville, Indiana, 1895
14. *E. G. Regon*
15. *Bart E. Linehan*, a tow boat
16. *T. T. Hillman*, named for owner of Hillman Iron Works, Thomas Tennessee Hillman
17. *L. P. Ewald*, named for president of Hillman Iron Works, and later named *Sam P. Jones*, for the evangelist

The Nashville Wharf in 1906. First Avenue is visible in the background. Courtesy of Tennessee State Library and Archives. Received in historical exchange from Pennsylvania History and Museum Commission.

18. *W. H. Cherry**
19. *James N. White*
20. *Julian Gracey*
21. *Josh V. Throop*
22. *L. T. Armstrong*
23 *John S. Bransford*
24. *E. B. Stahlman*
25. *John W. Thomas*
26. *Silverthorne*
27. *John Lunsden*
28. *P. D. Staggs*
29. *W. K. Hart*
30. *O. E. Stockell*
31. *William J. Cummins*
32. *Boliver H. Cooke*, original name of *J. P. Droulliard*
33. *Bermuda*, 1864

Tom Ryman Jr. built the *Robert Rhea* and the *Nashville*. Paul Ryman built *Jo Horton Fall.*

from Daisy's Book *by Daisy Ryman Coggins, date unknown*

Lights on the Character of My Father

by Daisy Ryman Coggins

I have mentioned the many magnolia trees that were a joy to Captain Ryman. We had deep snows in my early girlhood. It was always exciting on an early morning in the winter to look out at the deep snow, untrodden and a perfect carpet on the level spaces of lawn and many terraces leading down to Market Street (Second Avenue). All this purity of surface was soon marred by the tracks of old Mose (Moses McCutcheon), our handy man, because the Captain was sure to have told Mose to go to each magnolia tree and shake off the heavy snow. The broad leaves of these trees carried a heavy load of snow and there was danger of the limbs breaking.

In hot summer droughts Mose's duty was quite different, liberal watering of the magnolias and the elms on the sidewalk and indeed the whole place. All of us helped in this large task. It was big even with many water plugs to accommodate the hose.

One morning of very deep snow when Mose reported for duty the Captain said, "Mose, there's lots of suffering on Rolling Mill Hill this morning. Many people haven't enough fire." "Yes, Capt'n." "Go over there Mose and tell anybody who hasn't coal to come to my cellar with a tow sack. They can take a sack full home." "Yes, Capt'n." And there was a quick response. Before we were through breakfast they arrived with the sacks. The Captain smiled with satisfaction because his big cellar was full of coal. He bought it at low cost in summer from the Kentucky coal mines and when the boats came home from their summer of charter to the Ohio and Mississippi rivers they were laden with the coal. He thought the supply was inexhaustible but my mother was not quite so sure as the day wore on and the Negroes continued to come. At dinner time (midday dinner) she suggested they close the cellar door but my

29

father said no, they are cold and without fire. But by dark the cellar was empty after my mother saved enough to fill all the coal vases in the house. (It was heated by grate fires.) At supper Mother told the Captain, "We haven't enough coal for fires for the entire day." The Captain said meekly, because he knew that once more he had been very impractical as well as generous, "All right, I will order some coal from the local yards."

It was a very good thing that Mother was a woman of great practical sense. She was the balance wheel that his disposition needed. He recognized her value in this respect although it did not always restrain his extravagance, like the time he sent her a barrel of coconuts to make ambrosia which he liked very much. There was always a box of oranges in the house and always a barrel of apples. He bought everything wholesale. We had large storerooms—a barrel of sugar, fifty pounds of lard. This was a long time ago. Many people lived this way. In my early childhood there was a flour factory in the next block, he bought flour from his friend Noel there, in wooden barrels.

Mother, too, had the wholesale habit of buying some things. The country wagons passed all summer with fruits. She had regular men to buy from and we dreaded to see them drive up because it meant that all of us would spend the day on the back porch peeling fruit for preserves and pickles. She always bought a barrel of cider in the fall which she and she alone knew how to manage until it was apple vinegar, which she considered the best kind for pickles.

from Daisy's Book *by Daisy Ryman Coggins, date unknown*

Family Travel on the Ryman Steamboats

by Daisy Ryman Coggins

There were two hundred miles to where the Cumberland River flowed into the Ohio River. The scenery was varied and beautiful. Its shores touched Tennessee, Kentucky, and Indiana. After its confluence with the Ohio at Paducah, then Cairo and Shawnee Town, the great width of the river often looked like a lake and the scene was very beautiful, especially at sunset when favored passengers gathered in the pilothouse.

When the Ryman children were aboard they made it convenient to be in the pilothouse at four o'clock, because coffee was always served at that hour, and if the pilot was good natured he could speak to the steward through one of the three speaking tubes handy and order coffee for his visitors. He would also let a favorite child blow the whistle for a landing.

The great wheel never left his hands and his eyes had to watch many things, the changing currents of the river, the sand bars, a possible snag such as a dead tree caught in the soft bottom of the river. If a boat got aground it was a very difficult matter to get her free. The pilothouse visitors were very serious then and quiet, usually they went below.

Sometimes there were interesting people in the ladies-passengers' cabin, and often if there was no amusement inside there was something exciting outside. For example, if a lot of cattle were being brought aboard, it was as great as a circus to see the deck hands persuade reluctant cows to come aboard. Sometimes the cows resisted mightily and dragged the workmen back to the shore and wound the long ropes by which they were led around a convenient tree. They were very clever at giving all the trouble they could, but once aboard on the lower deck, safely installed and well fed, they were quiet and contented.

Other cargoes furnished amusement. Tobacco in huge heads were very heavy to handle and had to be eased down the gangplank with several men holding back while one man was in front with a huge block of wood with a long handle to keep the weight from running away from all of them. With all these precautions, I have seen a hogshead slip into the river. It would float and could be rescued, but by the hardest work and ingenuity. These heavy things were stored on the lower deck, of course, while lighter weight things were sometimes crowded along the guards, the name given the railings along the side doors of the staterooms and the pretty white balustrade which was the edge of the passenger deck. If these spaces were occupied by bags of peanuts, for instance, it was a strong temptation to make a hole in the tow sack and steal a handful.

I have seen light buggies loaded on the hurricane deck, this being the name of the roof of the passenger deck. Here was the texas (the sleeping quarters for the crew) and atop this the pilothouse. It was a

Statue of Tom Ryman at the east entrance to the Ryman Auditorium. Erected in 1994. Photograph by Gail Morris.

fascinating life. The rhythmic throb of the engines was pleasant to hear, the great wheel at the back was pleasant to watch as it threw the water up and over the wheel making a rainbow if the sun was shining, and moderate sized waves which followed in the wake of the steamer, then decreasing in size until they disappeared in the distance.

The Pontoon Bridge and the Elevator

by Daisy Ryman Coggins

The old Suspension Bridge spanning the Cumberland River and connecting Nashville with East Nashville was a thing of beauty. It was outlined against the sky and river like a giant spiderweb, hanging gracefully from the towers on either bank. These towers were tall and the threads of wire sloped downward towards the center where they closed in the floor of the bridge. A strong wind would sway the structure but it did not seem dangerous as indeed it was not until age and wear and tear of the rains and wind made it unsafe. I, for one was sorry to see it go down for it was beautiful to see from the high hill where our home was.

Its destruction had a personal interest to our family for my father had the contract of building and keeping in order the pontoon bridge to accommodate traffic while the new bridge was being built. This bridge was simply a series of small boats, side by side across the river, with a strong floor of heavy planks connecting them. When all this building was going on and the old bridge being destroyed, all at the same time, the scene was one of tremendous activity, noise and labor. Many Negroes were employed; they often sang as they worked. Pilings were sunk into the water where the rock piers for the new bridge were being built. It all looked dangerous, as indeed it was. After many weeks the pontoon bridge was finished. This time was strenuous for all of us because we had breakfast very early so that my father could be on the scene when work began. He was prompt, always ahead of time. All the rivermen in his employ were kept busy. He wanted all to be on hand when they arrived. One of the clerks on duty who slept upstairs over the office said the sound so early in the morning of Papa's horse and buggy rattling down Market Street was his signal to rise quickly. He would just have time to dress, seize a canoe at the wharf and be at the scene of action by the time Papa could drive across the bridge.

A Louisville firm had the contract for building the new bridge. The daughter of one of the important officials visited Nashville and became quite a belle in high society. She must have been beautiful if her picture was a good likeness. Mr. Harry Sheets, a local musician, composed a waltz in her honor and put her portrait, full size, on the title page. My music teacher, Mrs. Aline R. Blondner gave me this piece of music to learn. When I was working on something difficult and classical, she often gave me something simple and tuneful by way of encouragement. I can yet play "The Marie Waltz."

There are now four bridges across the Cumberland River at Nashville but none of them have the airy grace of the old Suspension Bridge.

The swift current of the river would frequently cause one of the little supporting boats of the pontoon bridge to break loose. This had to be corrected at once because traffic had to be stopped until repairs were made. If this happened at night our telephone would ring urgently and we would hear Papa hurrying out the door to see about the trouble.

One family joke has come down to us from this time. The pontoon was a toll bridge and one of the clerks who had a small office on one side of the river, and who collected tolls said it was anything but a pleasant job. One time a finely dressed lady, very handsome and imposing, riding in a fine carriage with a liveried driver, stopped and when this clerk came out to collect the toll, she became very angry and said, "This is an intolerable imposition. I absolutely refuse to pay it. Drive on, James!" The clerk was helpless. It is wonderful how many occasions we found to repeat the lady's indignant "Drive on, James." This clerk had a fine sense of humor and loved to tell this episode. If the lady concerned knew how many hearty laughs she made possible, how many far-fetched applications the words were made to fit, even to this day, would she have enjoyed so much her high handedness?

Whereas the building of the bridge had been a public project, the building of the Elevator was a private enterprise of my father. The same strenuous schedule was in order when the Elevator was built. It was for storing grain to suit the convenience of local customers.

There was long negotiation about a location. This was finally arranged with the approval of the L&N Railroad. A spur track was laid from the main line to the building. The building stood on the river bank and had to be in reach of the boats at all stages of water. Pilings had to be driven in the soft dirt bank of the river. The lines of the building were pleasing although they were strictly utilitarian. The upper loft was very high above the water and commanded a beautiful view of the river and the city. There was something restful about it.

An advertisement which appeared in the *Nashville American* on May 18, 1902, reads "Ryman Warehouse and Elevator. The new Ryman Warehouse is large and spacious and is located on the East bank of the Cumberland at the foot of Main street. The Elevator was constructed at a cost of $30,000, and has a capacity of 300,000 bushels of grain. The convenience and benefit derived from the elevator has facilitated river shipments materially. In connection with the elevator there is an inclined track on which cars are run alongside the boats, which enable them to transfer shipments to and from boat at an incredibly short time."

On March 30, 1905, three months after the death of my father, the elevator and warehouse burned. All was a total loss because it was not insured.

from Daisy's Book *by Daisy Ryman Coggins, date unknown*

Reminiscences of the Neighborhood

by Elizabeth Coggins Jones

A RYMAN GRANDCHILD'S COMPARISON
HYMAN'S GROCERY, NASHVILLE, TENNESSEE,
  ABOUT 1901, AND DRUID HILLS KROGER GROCERY,
  ATLANTA, GEORGIA, 1953

The Howard School children most likely would prefer Hyman's Grocery. The great open barrels of dill pickles were so easy to get at. Mrs. Hyman just reached in her hand and brought up a big, luscious pickle which tasted like food for the gods to the hungry child out at recess. The Ryman grandchildren later were of the opinion just expressed. They lived at the top of Rutledge Hill in the Ryman house.[1]

Breakfast was promptly at 6:30 a.m. There was a rising bell a half hour earlier so there was no excuse for any child to be late. We had to be completely dressed, ready for school, because immediately after breakfast Mother Bettie had family prayers in the living room; every child had to learn the Sunday School lesson for the next Sunday, every day learning a little more. By Saturday we were expected to really know it and were kept in until we could answer questions fairly well. On week days the great bell would end the family prayer meeting when everybody went to school.

There was a spring in the yard and several geese were always paddling around in the water. As soon as they spied Daisy walking rapidly toward the side gate they gave chase. They stretched their long necks and made a terrible hissing sound and Daisy fled for her life, expecting a bite from those yellow bills. They never did catch her before she was safe within the gate, where they always gave up. The Negroes at the cottage were always amused at this, always assured Daisy that the geese would not hurt her, but it was a terrifying experience.

But, I started out to compare Hyman's Grocery with a modern Kroger which I visited lately. The pickles are all locked up tight in clean glass jars, and there is no family life going on behind a closed door where Mr. Hyman, a Rabbi, prayed while Mrs. Hyman sold the groceries. There were always several Hyman children underfoot. In summer when watermelons covered a big part of the floor they sat on them and rode them astride. Mrs. Hyman always had a pleasant word for Mrs. Ryman and her children when they passed on their way to church.

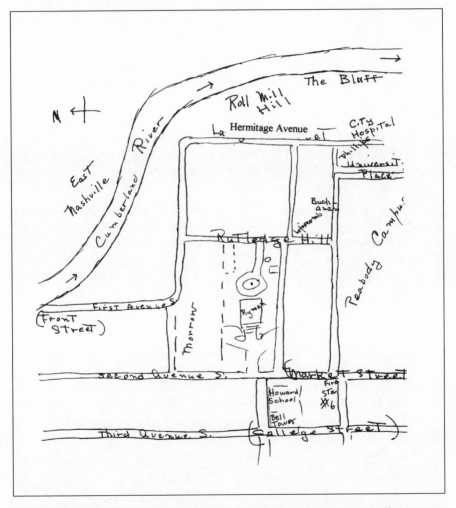

Rutledge Hill, drawn by Mrs. Thomas Proctor (Bennie Buchanan) in 1973 to identify places mentioned in Daisy's writing.

Captain Ryman's Home on Rutledge Hill

by Daisy Ryman Coggins

Tom Ryman's house at 514 South Market Street (now Second Avenue South) was built in 1885. The two-story Queen Anne style, Victorian frame sat in the middle of a terraced acre lot which included an Annex, summer house, carriage house with stables, a brick privy and a tennis court. He chose this site on Rutledge Hill because it commanded an excellent view of the river, the bridge and East Nashville beyond it. A great avenue of trees led down to the wharf before the Civil War and a well beside the road was freely used by travelers. My father reopened this well when he built his home, put a latticed house over it and it was the center of interest to the family. The water was cold and pure according to the city chemist's analysis. It was clear too, but no good for washing clothes. It was limestone and hard with alkali. This was unfortunate because Cumberland River water which came through the pipes in the house was very muddy. It had to be filtered for use at the table.

The yard was beautiful with many magnolias, many shrubs, many shade trees, and around the three sides of the property bordering the streets were elm trees unusually big when transplanted and each in a ten foot hole blasted from solid stone rock. These trees flourished in spite of everybody's prediction of failure. They and all the beauty of the yard were the pride and joy of Captain Tom Ryman.

The Ryman house had seven gables, two towers and many chimneys. They are vanished, gone with the wind,[1] as also the one square tower of the Morrow home, and also the great clock tower of Howard School. The clock is silent and also the great bell. Only the small central tower of the Baxter-Rutledge home still stands, looking

38

Ryman Home, 514 Market Street, Nashville, Tennessee. Photographed soon after its construction. The yard had been graded and terraced, but no landscaping had been done.

down at the Cumberland River which sweeps around Rolling Mill Hill, part of the wharf (where so much history has been made) and the bridges, to pass high cliffs and low fertile fields, past the beautiful town of Clarksville, Tennessee, once the largest tobacco market in the world.

There was a dangerous railroad bridge here and my father was always more or less uneasy until his boats had passed there. Very often then and always in high water he would call the wharf boat at Clarksville to learn whether a certain boat passed safely.

Ryman Home in 1890.

Historic markers of Captain Ryman's house. Photographs by Gail Morris.

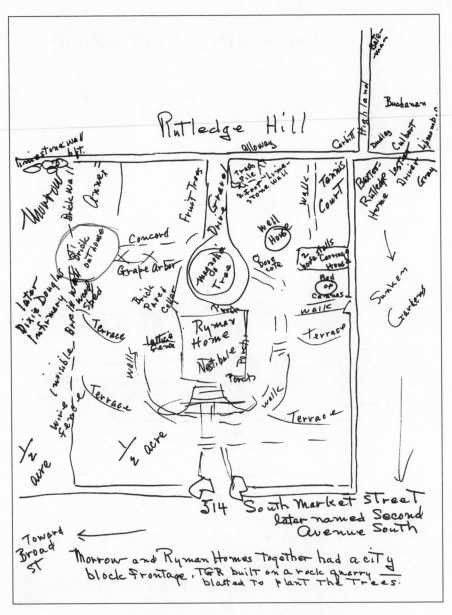

Plot plan of Ryman residence at 514 Market Street. Drawn by Mrs. Thomas Proctor (Bennie Buchanan) in 1973. Mrs. Proctor lived in the Ryman home following the death of her mother in 1912 until she was grown.

Captain Ryman's Business Philosophy

Recorded by an unnamed family member on the back of a laundry list dated June 28, 1892, and among Daisy Ryman Coggins' papers is the following interview with Captain Tom Ryman on his business philosophy.

Learn your business thoroughly. Keep at one thing; in no wise change. Always be in haste, but never in a hurry. Observe system in all you do and undertake. Whatever is worth doing at all is worth doing well. One today is worth two tomorrows. Be self reliant. Do not take too much advise but rather depend on yourself. Never fail to keep your appointments nor to be punctual to the minute. Never be idle, but keep your hands or mind usefully employed except when sleeping. Use charity with all. Be ever generous in thought and deed. Help others along life's thorny path. Make no haste to be rich, remember that small and steady gains give competency and tranquility of mind. He that ascends the ladder must take the lowest round. All who are above were once below.

There are two things each of which he will seldom fail to discover who seeks for it in earnest: the knowledge of what he ought to do, and a plausible pretext to do what he likes.

Life's real heroes and heroines are those who bear their own burdens bravely and give a helping hand to those around them.

Innocence is like a flower which withers when touched and blooms not again though watered with tears.

Amusements are necessary in order to give a completeness to life.

PART 3

OTHER
WRITINGS

Nashville Banner, *November 28, 1926*

Old Times on the Upper Cumberland

by Captain J. S. Tyner

TYNER'S REMINISCENCES

I was born in Chattanooga, Tennessee in the year 1847 and took to the water like a duck when very young. My first steamboating was in the year 1858 on the steamer *Little Tennessee* (Capt. Jack Doss, Master) plying between Chattanooga and Knoxville. The following year, 1858, Captain Tom Ryman, then only 15 years old, employed me to go with him to his fishing boat which was lying at the mouth of Chickamauga Creek where the great battle by that name was fought later. The job assigned me was that of digging worms. Besides Tom Ryman there were three others, making four fishermen for whom I had to supply worms, digging them from the bank of the river.

Tom Ryman had been started out in the fishing business at the age of 15 by his father, John Ryman, who then came to Nashville to sell the fish and handle the financial part of the business. Previous to that John Ryman had been engaged in the steamboat business on the Cumberland River with his brother Charles Ryman, but they went broke in the business. John Ryman then borrowed money and went to Chattanooga. But before going to Nashville John Ryman put up ice for medical purposes only. This was before he put up his son in the fishing business.

There was a high bluff just above the present upper bridge at Chattanooga and the sun never shines in the water at the foot of this bluff. John Ryman placed a flat boat at the foot of this bluff with a few inches of water in it. This water would freeze overnight, and the next day he would pump two or three more inches of water into the boat on top of the ice and let it freeze the following night. The process would be repeated until the ice became thick enough to put up.

44

IN THE ARMY

After fishing around Chickamauga Creek for several months we dropped down to Shell Mound, Alabama, on the Tennessee River. It was while we were at Shell Mound that war was declared between the North and the South. I enlisted in the war and went to Camp Cummins at Knoxville and afterwards was stationed at Cumberland Gap during the Summer. While stationed at Cumberland Gap our regiment, which was the 19th Tennessee, went through into Kentucky to the salt works and brought back 90 wagon loads of salt. Late in fall of 1861 we came through to Mill Springs where we put up winter quarters of logs and boards, and in the Spring following, the Union soldiers were encroaching on us, so we went out to Fishing Creek to stop them. Instead of our stopping them, they drove us back to our winter quarters at Mill Springs.

In our retreat to our winter quarters it was necessary to cross the river and the sergeant came around during the night and made it plain that it was also necessary to be quiet about it otherwise we would be heard and captured. I was drummer boy at the time and they would not even allow me to bring my drums. A little later I was glad of this for it was hard for me to pull through the mud myself. At this time a Capt. Spillers, who was in charge of a cavalry company, had taken possession of the steamer *Noble Ellis* which had come there with a load of supplies for the army. This cavalry company was made up in part of experienced steamboat men so Capt. Spillers took charge of the boat that night and agreed to ferry us all over provided he was permitted to take his cavalry horses across on the first trip. This was agreed to and the cavalry horses and soldiers were ferried across, but a number of artillery horses and heavy artillery were captured by the Union forces. After ferrying us across the river this boat was fired by the Confederates and drifted down the river sinking, I believe at the head of Forbush Island, and her engines are lying on the bank there, or were a few years ago.

I got my discharge from the army just after the Battle of Shiloh. The discharge was given me on account of disability and youthful age. I returned home to Chattanooga and never felt physically able to reenlist.

COMES TO NASHVILLE

Soon after the Battle of Chickamauga [September 19, 1863] I came to Nashville where I again met Capt. Tom Ryman and went with him to Decatur, Alabama, to the two fishing boats he had at that place. After remaining at Decatur for a few months I returned to Nashville sick and made my home with Capt. Tom's father, as one of the family. As soon as I felt well enough I secured a job as watchman on the steamer *David Hughes*, one of Uncle Tom Leek's boats. Charles Yarbrough (better known as Bud Yarbrough) was cub pilot on this boat at this time. After that I went on the *Kate Roberts* which was engaged in bringing army supplies to Nashville from Cincinnati and Pittsburgh for the Federal army.

After working on this boat a few trips, Capt. Tom Ryman wanted me to go to Johnsonville, Tennessee, and look after two fishing boats which he still had at that place, while he went to Decatur, Alabama, to look after two of his fishing boats there. After we had finished up the year's fishing Capt. Tom Ryman bought his first steamboat, the *Alpha*, and made enough money the first two years operating her on the Cumberland River to build the steamer *Eddyville*. I got sick and had to give up fishing, but after getting well I started a business of my own, buying and selling fish.

After operating this business a few years Capt. T. Ryman sold me a half interest in the *Eddyville*. We ran her as partners for one year and sold her to Capt. David Hughes and built the first steamer *B. S. Rhea*. This was in 1878. We ran the *B. S. Rhea* for eight years and then rebuilt her retaining the same name.

THE SECOND *RHEA*

We built the *B. S. Rhea* in 1886. She was also operated by us for eight years and then sold to some parties at Cincinnati, Ohio. Afterwards she was laid up at Sedamsville, a suburb of Cincinnati where she burned. On one occasion during high water while we were operating the second *Rhea* after landing at Canton the boat went out on a flat place on a swell or wave and when the swell left her she was hard aground with the river falling. She was left high and dry with her stern pointing out over the river and the wheel over about twelve feet of water. I had one of the derrick sticks sawed in two making two strong posts which I had inserted under each cylinder timber under the shaft to support the stern otherwise the boat would have broken in two. The boat was afterwards jacked up and launched back into the river. When this launching was begun the stern of the vessel was about 25 feet from the water, due to the river falling. When everything was in readiness to do the launching a jack screw was set against her stern and the steamer *W. K. Phillips* gave her a pull from the river side, after which she slid into the river without any trouble. . . .

OTHER BOATS

Capt. Tom Ryman also had an interest in the steamer *C. W. Anderson* which was built from the *Old Julia No. 2.* His partner in this vessel was Capt. John Crouch. I think the *C. W. Anderson* was built in the year 1877. This boat was afterwards sold to the authorities of Louisiana and converted into a convict vessel.

About the year 1896, I went on the steamer *Alex Perry* on the Evansville-Nashville trade. She was burned while lying at the Evansville wharfboat while the steamer was drifting down the river burning.

After this the steamer *H. W. Buttorff* was built and operated in the Nashville-Paducah trade. This boat was afterwards sold to the Lees of Memphis, Tennessee, and is at the present time operating as an excursion boat named *Princess.*

ACCIDENT AT CLARKSVILLE

On one occasion while operating the *Buttorff*, I have forgotten the date, we were nearing the Clarksville bridge, going downstream. He blew the necessary signals and the bridge was opened by the tender. A train approaching from the west side of the river for some reason failed to notice the signal indicating the bridge was open, but kept coming, and the engine, mailcar, baggage car, plunged into the river from the bridge drowning two members of the crew. My recollection is they were the engineer and express messenger. The fireman and three others got out alive. The baggage master, I think it was, and some of the other members of the crew hammered on the windows of the submerged baggage car, finally breaking out and climbed on top of the car, from which they were rescued by the ferryman at Clarksville. When these cars plunged

Thomas Green Ryman (1841–1904).

off the bridge, the trucks became detached and the cars floated down river, about four inches showing above the water. After we had unloaded the *Buttorff* we went on down the river and caught these cars and tied them up at the bank. We also recovered several pieces of baggage and express matter which were floating on the river.

ON THE MISSISSIPPI

Fishing and steamboating together I was associated with Capt. T. Ryman about 45 years. After his death I was identified with the new Ryman line. The president of this new line, Mr. Frank Lester, went to New Orleans and at a sale of a Red River line bought steamers *Electra, Red River,* and *W. T. Scovell.* This was, I think, about 1905. We borrowed Capt. W. T. Hunter from St. Louis and Tennessee River Packet Co. of St. Louis to go to New Orleans and bring these boats to Paducah, Kentucky. On this trip wind, fog, rain, ice, and everything conceivable happened to delay the trip. There were several narrow escapes from losing the boats. The trip consumed 23 days and was such a hard trip Capt. Hunter lost ten pounds actual weight as he had only a single crew and was attempting to run night and day with the three boats leashed together. . . . This fleet of three boats finally landed at Paducah. I went to Paducah from Nashville and took the *Scovell* and *Electra* to Mount City, Indiana, for repairs . . . and Capt. Hunter went back to St. Louis and Tennessee Packet Company as master of steamer *Clyde.*

The steamer *Red River* was sold back to Mississippi River interest, the *W. T. Scovell* was operated a short time and then sold to some parties in Vicksburg, Mississippi, where her boilers exploded, killing 3 or 4 members of her crew according to my recollections. The steamer *Electra* was operated by the Ryman line for several years and later sold to Mobile, Alabama, parties where she afterwards burned.[1]

The Colorful Eighties in Nashville, *printed serially in the* Nashville Banner, *date unknown*

Last Days of Real Steamboating on the Cumberland

by M. B. Morton

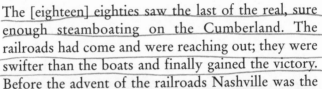

16

The [eighteen] eighties saw the last of the real, sure enough steamboating on the Cumberland. The railroads had come and were reaching out; they were swifter than the boats and finally gained the victory. Before the advent of the railroads Nashville was the receiving and distribution point of a large steamboat territory. Great sidewheelers ran on the rivers to New Orleans, St. Louis, Pittsburgh and intervening points. An immense amount of cotton was shipped from Nashville by boat. Decatur, Alabama, sent cotton to Nashville by wagon, because of the Muscle Shoals it would not be shipped on the Tennessee River. A great wagon yard for the teams and wagons occupied an open space in South Nashville. Many of the buildings still standing in the business section were then cotton warehouses.

In the eighties, though river trade was not what it had been, it was still great. The wharf was a busy place, piled with products and merchandise of every description. The steamboats had become sternwheelers, so that they could navigate the shallow streams, but they were doing business. The picturesque Negro deckhands, and roustabouts, in charge of a profane mate, lent color to the scene at the landing, as they hurried back and forth, singing and laughing, and paying little or no attention to the mate's voluble oaths and threats. The later swore by note, and seemed to think it a necessary part of the routine.

All day and all night the hoarse whistle of the boats could be heard. Before they left they whistled to notify belated passengers and deckhands they were about to start, and when they arrived they whistled to let the "night-hawk" hacks know they were coming with passengers; and to let the local roustabouts know they were coming with freight to be unloaded. When a boat reached the landing, the "night-hawks" and the roustabouts would be there.

STEAMBOAT MUSIC

It was the custom of all the Negro hands to gather on the swinging gangplank as the boats backed out and started on their journey and sing boat songs and spirituals, while a leader gesticulated and led the singing. No one who has stood on the Woodland Street Bridge as a steamboat passed down stream and has witnessed the scene described and heard the wonderful chanting of these natural born musicians will ever forget the thrill of it.

The steamboat season opened about the middle of November and lasted until about August 1st. During the low-water period between these dates these boats went to the Ohio River and took the place of boats of deeper draft until the fall rise came.

The main steamboat lines during this time were the Cincinnati and Nashville Packet Company, the Cincinnati and Pittsburgh, the Nashville and Burnside Packet Company, and the famous Ryman line. The principal products handled were corn, tobacco, wheat, and all kinds of merchandise, pig iron and iron manufactures from Pittsburgh. Coal by tow boats was brought from Pittsburgh for the Nashville Gas Company. Coal was also brought from Poplar Mountain Mines, thirty miles west of Burnside, Kentucky, and from the Cumberland Coal Company at Burnside. It was brought in broad-horn barges. The Cumberland Coal was such like that from Pittsburgh.

Merchandise from Eastern cities was picked up by the boats at Ohio River points. Livestock was brought to Nashville from up and down the Cumberland; and mules were shipped from Nashville to New Orleans and other Southern markets.

Passenger business on the river was also of large dimensions. An enormous emigration went from Kentucky and Tennessee to Texas. Through tickets would be sold to them, and the last part of the trip would be by rail.

Travel by boat was fascinating. There were good bands and bars, and in the evening dancing, card playing and other forms of amusement were engaged in. The Captain and Chief Clerk were the masters of ceremony. They saw that the passengers were introduced to one another, that those who wished to dance had partners. They looked after the comfort of all and saw that everything was properly conducted. These men were Chesterfieldian in their manners; they had known many and varied experiences and were generally fine conversationalists.

CAPTAIN T. G. RYMAN

The dominating figure on the river for many years was Captain Thomas G. Ryman. He had little education but a good mind. He was tall, angular, raw boned and powerful. He was a man of strong personality and marked peculiarities. He amassed a comfortable fortune, though primarily not a money seeker. He had physical and moral courage and his energy knew no bounds. When he started to do a thing it was as good as an accomplished fact. The Ryman Auditorium is a monument to his persistence and untiring religious zeal, for which he was noted during the last half of his life. He wanted a great auditorium where Sam Jones and other great preachers could hold services without cost. He made a liberal donation himself, and then entered into a canvass that knew no let up until the building was finished.

The night before the auditorium was to be dedicated he visited the office of the *Nashville Banner* and the *American* newspapers, and told each of the reporters and editors who had aided him in his undertaking to go around to Rowen's tailoring establishment, order a fifty-dollar suit and charge it to him. A fifty-dollar suit in those days was considered rather extravagant.

He had professed religion while Sam Jones was conducting a tent meeting on the southwest corner of Broadway and Eighth Avenue, where Davis Drug Store now stands. Prior to that time he had taken little interest in religion, having concentrated his energies on steamboats and politics. After his conversion he lead an exemplary life, and the contrast was so great that it gave rise to many apocryphal stories as to the wild, hilarious life Captain Ryman lived in his younger days. He was, however, always honest and always charitable. He was not a heavy drinker nor a gambler, though it was a fact that he won $12,000 on Grover Cleveland during his first race for the presidency. He was an enthusiastic Democrat and actively interested, heart and soul, in this race.

It has often been said that after his conversion he destroyed all the bars on his steamboats and poured the liquor into the river. This is a good story, but unfortunately is not sustained by the facts. Captain

Ryman did not own the bars on his steamboats. They were leased to the men who conducted them. He did, however, notify these men that he would lease no more bar room privileges; and in this way the Ryman line became dry.[1]

Raising Money For Tabernacle Galleries

RAISE MONEY FOR THE GALLERIES
WORK FOR THE GOSPEL TABERNACLE ASSUMES A VERY PRACTICAL SHAPE

The work in behalf of getting the galleries put into the Gospel Tabernacle is beginning in earnest.

The committee appointed to see after the matter of raising the needed funds met yesterday morning at Gen. W. H. Jackson's office. Capt. J. B. O'Bryan sent in a communication setting forth that, despite his heartiest sympathy with the work, his arduous duties in the work connected with the Confederate reunion prevented his serving as Chairman. Gen. Jackson was then unanimously elected Chairman, and he formulated the following call for a meeting at 11 o'clock this morning:

"By virtue of my appointment as Chairman and with the assistance and concurrence of the committee I do hereby appoint the following general committee of ladies and gentlemen to assist in the work of soliciting subscriptions in order that we may complete the galleries at the very earliest time. Your Chairman would most earnestly impress upon each member the importance and necessity for very prompt action and to this end hereby calls a meeting at the Tabernacle at 11 A.M. February 16.

"I would further state that while I designate this committee I would urge upon every lady and gentleman in the city who feels an interest in this matter, which is so absolutely essential to the proper entertainment of the large assemblages that will be in our city during the Centennial, and especially the large gathering of Confederate Veterans to meet here June 22, 23 and 24, to meet with us at the Tabernacle and aid in every possible way to raise the amount necessary within the next few days as we barely have time now to let our contracts and have the work completed by June next, as it will require eighty days to complete the work after the contracts are let.

Ryman and Jones families on the steps of the Ryman house. Also present are members of the revival quartet and French horn player. Tom Ryman is standing in the back row, second from the left. Sam Jones is seated below the French horn player. The families became good friends.

"So, I would respectfully urge upon all the members of the committee and all who are interested to attend this meeting. Any who have not contributed and desire to do so can telephone today Mr. S. A. Cunningham, Secretary, No. 298, and he can report the same to the general meeting. Very respectfully. W. H. JACKSON, Chairman."[. . .]

Nor are the women idle. A goodly number of them met yesterday morning in the lecture room of the First Presbyterian Church to devise ways and means for assisting in the work of putting the gallery in the Tabernacle. Mrs. E. H. East was elected President and Mrs. Annie Scurers Gilchrist was elected Secretary of the organization, which is to be known as the Ladies' Tabernacle Circle. The meeting was opened with prayer by Mrs. Bang, and "Where He Leads Me I Will Follow" was sung. Mrs. Turner announced a proposition from Mr. Jones to give a new lecture that he will prepare especially for the occasion, and the offer was unanimously accepted. Mrs. Nat Baxter proposed that he be induced to give the lecture as soon as possible to make the interest more intense.

Dr. Vance came in and spoke encouragingly saying: "Ladies. If you will, you can raise $2,000 by this lecture." Mrs. Ryman gave an interesting talk about the Tabernacle which aroused the ladies to renewed enthusiasm in the work. Mrs. Crutcher suggested that in addition to the lecture a sacred concert be given by local talent in the near future. Mrs. Turner, Mrs. Ryman, and Mrs. Baskette were appointed a committee to meet Mr. Jones at the train Wednesday morning when he will be en route from Atlanta and ascertain the date at which he will deliver the lecture.

The meeting then adjourned to meet again next Thursday morning at 10 o'clock in the lecture room of the First Presbyterian Church. All ladies who feel an interest in the work are earnestly urged to be present at that meeting. It is also urged that as many of the ladies as possible attend the meeting this morning at 11 o'clock.

The Reunion Club has appointed the following ladies to take active part in the movement, and especially asks them to be present at the meeting at the Tabernacle this morning at 11 o'clock.

Mesdames John Overton, Ellen Marshall, I. M. Clark, H. L. Craighead, E. D. McNeilly, Mary P. McGuire, Mary Smith, W. J. McMurray, Anne E. Snyder, Harry W. Evans, M. C. Goodlett, J. R. Richardson, I. K. Chase, J. H. Fall, B. B. Allen, John C. Gant, Nat Gooch, W. R. Elliston, Novella Marks, Misses Mackie Hardison, Adrie McMurray, Margaret Eakin, Leonora O'Bryan, Annie D. Richardson, Elizabeth Jackson.

A hearty invitation is also extended to all workers in the Christian Endeavor ranks to attend this morning's meeting, as the putting in of the galleries will come in most opportunely for the great meeting of the International Convention of Christian Endeavor Societies in Nashville in 1898.

Captain Ryman's Generous Offer

MEN AND WOMEN ORGANIZED

SAM JONES WILL LECTURE FOR THE FUND—SEVERAL
BODIES UNITED IN A MEETING AT THE TABERNACLE
THIS MORNING

To the Citizens of Nashville: When I was converted in the tent on Broad Street eleven years ago I loved everybody. The night following I saw the multitudes standing and turned away, and it was then that I conceived the idea of the Tabernacle. I drew a pencil sketch and met with others at Col. E. W. Cole's residence. The Y.M.C.A. building was discussed and decided upon, thus ruling out the Tabernacle for the time being. But at the meeting the year following, in the Amusement Hall, it took a new start and we raised on five years' time $20,000. Afterwards, after days of hunting among real estate men, we bought the lot on which the Tabernacle stands—central land with no street cars passing the building to annoy the meeting. We built the foundation and put a tent over it, and held another meeting, seating it with round blocks and planks. Then we raised the walls and put an $11,000 steel truss roof on, which weighed 110 tons, spanning 118 feet by 180 feet. Other meetings followed and scores have been blessed and great good accomplished. We have seated it nicely.

I have prayed to God when most people were asleep. I have worked for this Tabernacle hard for ten years; have neglected my business and paid money out for it liberally; so much have I done this that many people thought I had plenty of money. That is a mistake; I had my heart in it, though, just like I have for sinners with our Gospel Wagon and the boards around the city bearing scripture verses. I have done all I could, but here is the situation now with the Tabernacle.

There is an $18,000 debt on it; the gallery is badly needed. I am carrying it for $2,400. It will not float unless the citizens of Nashville will lift the debt, put in the gallery, put on a slate roof and put in heaters. I will donate the $2,400 I am carrying and give $1,000.

Union Gospel Tabernacle (Ryman Auditorium) shortly after it was constructed in 1897.

We have a meeting of the committee today at 11 o'clock at the Tabernacle to discuss ways and means to put in the gallery at least. All friends to the enterprise are earnestly requested to be present.

Respectfully, T. G. RYMAN

Capt. Tom Ryman's Work on the River and for Religion

There is possibly not a man in Nashville who has done more for the upbuilding of the city in his own particular line than has Capt. Thomas G. Ryman, the head of the Ryman line of steamers. In a river career extending over thirty-five years Capt. Ryman has had built for his own use twenty-two large steamboats, and he has owned or controlled eight others, making a total of thirty large boats, all of which were run in and out of Nashville, up and down the Cumberland and into the Ohio, Tennessee and Mississippi Rivers.

While Capt. Ryman is well known for his success as a steamboat owner and operator, he is much better known as a "Tabernacle builder." Everybody in Nashville who takes the least interest in religion or keeps abreast of current events knows of the sacrifices, both of time and money, made by Capt. Ryman to building the capacious and handsome Union Gospel Tabernacle now standing on Summer just above Broad Street.

Capt. Ryman was born in the southern portion of this city in 1841 and remained here until he was 10 years of age, when his parents removed to Chattanooga. He remained there until he was grown, returning here at the age of 20 years, where he has remained continuously since. He engaged in business as a fisherman, plying his trade diligently for seven years. At the end of that time, or in 1867, he had accumulated some money and bought the steamer *Alpha*, which ran out of New Orleans [when he purchased it]. The boat was 150 feet in length and 30 feet in width. He brought her here and ran successfully in the upper river the first season. Later he ran in the lower river and into the Ohio River. At the end of two years she was dismantled and he built the *Eddyville*, one of the most successful boats ever on this river.

CAPT. RYMAN'S BOATS

Captain Ryman later built and bought the following boats—*Shippers Own, B. H. Cooke, J. S. Bransford, E. B. Stahlman, Bermuda, C. W. Anderson, 2 B. S. Rheas, J. P. Droulliard, W. H. Cherry, J. H. Hillman, E. G. Regon, Alex Perry, W. K. Phillips, P. D. Staggs, H. W. Buttorff, Bob Dudley, J. B. Richardson, Dover, Julian Gracey, R. Dunbar, L. P. Ewald, I. T. Rhea, Sam Fowler, Ashland City, L. T. Armstrong, Silverthorne,* and *Josh V. Throop.*

Captain Thos. M. Gallagher has been associated with Captain Ryman in the steamboat business for twenty-five years or more and has done his full part in making the Ryman lines the success they have been. Captain Gallagher was born in Louisville in 1856 but came to Nashville with his parents at the age of four years and has been here continuously since. When he was a very young man he began to follow in the footsteps of his father, who was a riverman. He entered a local steamboat agency as office boy, gradually working his way up until he was made third clerk on one of the boats. His ability was recognized in a short time and he was jumped over the heads of some of his superiors and made master of the boat. He continued to run in that capacity for about twenty years.

Capt. Gallagher was appointed to his present position as general freight and passenger agent of the Ryman lines in 1888. To merely say that he has filled the position with ability would be putting it too mildly for his full worth to be appreciated, for there is no better "freight getter" in the business than Capt. Gallagher. He is a good mixer and is popular wherever he goes. He always has a pleasant smile for everybody and a kind word for all of his friends. He is a jolly good fellow when he meets a jolly good fellow and strictly business when he meets a business man for a business talk.

HELP NASHVILLE

The policy of the Ryman lines, under Capt. Ryman and Gallagher, has always been to help in the upbuilding of Nashville, as the two gentlemen recognize the fact that the better condition this city is in the more it will be to the steamboat lines.

It is a well-known fact that the Ryman lines have never charged exorbitant freight rates. The tendency is rather to recede them and to run in low water as long as possible.

Ryman Auditorium when the Grand Ole Opry was held there.
Courtesy of the Tennessee State Library and Archives.

It has always been a rule of the company never to charge freight on anything that is to be used in connection with a church, even brick being hauled when requested.

The company also has an arrangement with the Chamber of Commerce whereby all merchants from points up the river coming to Nashville are given free transportation in both directions and all Nashville drummers traveling in that territory are accommodated in the same way. The wholesalers of the city desire to increase trade in that section, and the steamboat company is aiding in the effort, knowing that the returns after a larger trade is established will more than justify the present outlay.

CAPT. RYMAN'S GREATEST WORK

Capt. Ryman first conceived the idea of a Gospel Tabernacle for all denominations when he was converted at the first meeting held in this city by Rev. Sam Jones. On that night, after Capt. Ryman had professed religion, he went into the outskirts of the crowd in and around the tent then being used, to find some of his friends he thought should be talked with. The tent was more than filled and he found some of these friends crowded back more than ten feet on the outside. It was just at that moment that he conceived the idea of a Tabernacle for all denominations that would be amply large to accommodate the largest crowd.

Capt. Ryman suggested the idea to Mr. Jones that night. Later it was talked over at length by those interested, but it was finally decided that it would be best to postpone the idea for the time being, as the Young Men's Christian Association building was at the time being pushed forward and it was not thought advisable to put another public enterprise forward at the same time. The Y.M.C.A. building in question is the present handsome structure standing on Church street just below Cherry.

The Tabernacle matter was taken up in earnest when Mr. Jones visited the city the second time. The last night of Mr. Jones' second meeting he put the matter before the public and in thirty minutes had raised $21,000 to be paid in five installments. Mr. Jones thought it would be best to buy the Broad Street Amusement Hall for the purpose and the subscriptions were made with this idea in view. Later some of the largest subscribers met with Capt. Ryman and he prevailed on them to accept his first idea and erect a building that would answer all purposes for years to come. The vacant lot on the corner of Vine and Broad streets was first considered and later other lots that were centrally located, but just off of a street car line. The owner of the lot finally selected agreed to sell it on the same terms that the subscriptions were made and his proposition was accepted.

Building Begun

It was some time after this before work was actually begun on the building. The foundation was first put in and two feet of brick work laid.

The funds on hand were exhausted by that time and work had to be stopped and it was two years before anything more was done. Capt. Ryman became very anxious for the work to go ahead and consulted many of his friends. Finally O. F. Noel told Capt. Ryman to go to the banks and borrow money with which to continue the work and he [Mr. Noel] would stand by him. Capt. Ryman borrowed $12,000 from the banks and Mr. Jones came for another meeting and raised an additional $20,000 on the same five-year time as the first subscriptions. Work was then resumed and the building completed. This does not include the gallery nor the seats in the building, these being put in later. The old rough seats used in the tent were continued in use in the Tabernacle for some time.

Lifting the Debt

When the roof was on the building its promoters were a good many thousand dollars in debt and it has required a Herculean effort since then to lift the debt. Capt. Ryman and others then turned their attention to raising money for clearing the debt. How many miles Capt. Ryman walked, and how much talking he did in trying to raise money for the Tabernacle will never be known. He raised on the streets through his individual efforts $10,000, and is now just as anxious to get the matter cleared up as he had been from the beginning.

An *American* reporter talked with Capt. Ryman in getting some of the facts given above. The Captain wanted everybody but himself to have credit for what has been done and said continuously while being questioned that this man or that man should be given credit for this thing or that. He had to be pinned right down to get out of him what he did, and he was inclined to think of all others first and himself last. This article concerns only the Captain and there would not be space for going into details concerning others.

Capt. Ryman stated that $3,000 in cash would now practically put the Tabernacle out of debt. The debt at present is $11,000, but the Treasurer has in his possession good notes to the value of $8,000 and more than that of old notes that cannot be collected. After this debt is cleared Capt. Ryman says a slate roof should be put on the building that would cost $2,000. This means that $5,000 would practically pay all debts and put the entire building in strictly first-class shape. As it is, the structure is a monument to the earnest effort of a devoted Christian man.

PART 4

TOM RYMAN'S
DEATH & FUNERAL

Good Summary

The Death of Captain Tom Ryman Sr.

Capt. Thomas Green Ryman, in his time the greatest steamboat man the Cumberland River ever knew, passed quietly away at 3:45 Friday afternoon at his home, 514 South Second Avenue (Market Street). Capt. Ryman had been in failing health for two years but only on Tuesday did he take to his bed.

Revs. Sam Jones and George Stewart will reach here tomorrow morning and will conduct funeral services at 2:30 o'clock tomorrow afternoon at the Union Gospel Tabernacle, which will ever remain as a memorial to Capt. Ryman. Capt. Ryman leaves a wife and seven children.

Capt. Ryman was born in South Nashville October 12, 1841, and was 63 years old at the time of his death. When he was 10 years old his family removed to Chattanooga, where he remained until 1861, when the family returned to Nashville. He was the son of Capt. John Ryman, the pioneer of Cumberland River steamboat men. He was the oldest of six children, one of whom was drowned when a child. The others are living.

Capt. Ryman married Miss Mary Elizabeth Baugh, of Franklin, on Feb. 12, 1869, by whom he had seven children, all of whom survive him. They are T. G. Ryman Jr., Mesdames Gus and Roll Coggins, of Canton, Georgia, Mrs. Walter Barton, of Atlanta, Mrs. J. C. Buchanan, Miss Georgia Ryman, and Paul Ryman of Nashville. His brother, John C. Ryman, and his sisters Mesdames Biese, Virgie Moore, and Francis Carell, reside in Chattanooga and are here for the funeral.

Capt. Ryman began his business life with his father in the steamboat business. Unfortunate investments financially ruined the older Ryman, and he died penniless in 1864,[1] leaving Capt. Ryman, then 23 years old, to support his mother, one brother and three sisters, to do which he set manfully to work. Although he directed his energies in humble channels, he kept the family together, weathering financial shoals and evidencing those sterling qualities and the business acumen which formed the foundations of his successes of later years.

In 1865 he had accumulated enough money to purchase the steamer *Alpha*, which was then running out of New Orleans. He brought it to the Cumberland and plied it on both the upper and lower rivers. He had strong opposition and his competitors, realizing that they individually could not cope with him, pooled their interests in an endeavor to force him from the river. They failed, however, while the young steamboatman made money, and in 1869 he built the steamer *Eddyville*, dismantling the *Alpha* and using her engines in the new boat. He sold the hull of the *Alpha* and it was used for some years as a barge on the Ohio.

From that time his business grew steadily and he kept adding to his fleet. In 1875 he organized the People's Line which plied between Nashville and Burnside. The name of this line was later changed to the Nashville & Burnside Packet Company and in 1880 he organized the Nashville, Paducah and Cairo Packet Company; in 1882 he organized the Nashville & Evansville Packet Company. In 1885 these three lines were consolidated into the Ryman Line, retaining their individuality as "divisions" of the Ryman Line instead of "packet companies." At this time he owned seven boats on the river.

In all, from the time he purchased the *Alpha*, in 1865, to his retirement, a few weeks ago, Capt. Ryman owned or controlled 35 steamboats, the largest number ever owned or controlled by any man or firm which has operated on the Cumberland River.

The corporation which acquired the interest of Capt. Ryman recently still retains the name of the Ryman Line.

CONVERTED BY SAM JONES

Capt. Ryman was converted at the first meeting held in Nashville by Rev. Sam Jones at the tent, corner of Spruce and Broad Streets. At a meeting held later that night he suggested the idea of a Union Gospel Tabernacle. Later $21,000 was pledged to purchase the Amusement Hall on Broad Street. Capt. Ryman objected to the purchase of this, however, and his idea of a large tabernacle prevailed terminating in the erection of the Tabernacle on North Fifth Avenue (Summer Street), which will ever be associated with his name.

Capt. Ryman was a devout member of Elm Street Church, but, although identified with the Methodist denomination, he was not a sectarian in the real sense of the word. His idea in erecting a large taber-

nacle capable of seating 6,000 or 7,000 people was thereby to secure the cooperation of both the Jews and Gentiles, and bring mankind closer together in gospel meetings and so uplift all. He was himself a strong believer in the teachings and divinity of Christ, and earnestly desired and worked for the obliteration of denominational lines between the followers of the Man of Galilee.

His charity was proverbial. Neither white or black was ever turned a suppliant away. Tales of want and suffering brought the tears of sympathy to his eyes. His heart went always out to suffering humanity, and he never tired of extending financial aid for the amelioration of suffering and want. His greatest charities were in the nature of burying the dead and caring for the poor, but there was no ostentation about his giving. Those who were closest to him knew of them only by chance, and if mentioned in his presence he would dismiss the subject. If a darkey who had been in his employ died he saw that he had a Christian burial, and that his family did not suffer.

Northwestern view of monument on Ryman Lot at Mount Olivet Cemetery. The carving of a steamboat symbolizes his steamboating career.

A DESERVED TRIBUTE

Capt. T. M. Gallagher, who for 27 years has been closely associated with him, during 20 years of which he has been his confidential adviser in business, religious and all other matters, said Friday: "He was one of the most generous men in Nashville. He had a heart that filled his breast, and I never knew him to refuse any one who approached him, nor did I ever know of him to give grudgingly. He never hesitated. When charity was asked or when he realized it was needed his hand sought his purse."

Since professing religion Capt. Ryman has never allowed a drop of intoxicants to be carried or sold on his boats. This is true probably of no other steamboat line in the country and aroused astonishment when the order was issued by Capt. Ryman. He was always a friend of religion and would not charge one cent for carrying any freight to be used for erecting church buildings, even bricks being transported free by him. There is scarcely a church in Nashville that he has not helped at one time or another.

Capt. Ryman left an estate, according to papers in a Chancery Court case, involving the appointment of his wife as guardian, of $146,000 net, it reaching a gross total of $181,000, with liabilities of something under $35,000.

Detail of the steamboat carving on the Ryman monument. Photograph by Gail Morris.

Nashville Banner, *Saturday Evening, December 24, 1904*

Capt. Ryman's Last Voyage

CROSSED THE DARK RIVER YESTERDAY AFTERNOON
FUNERAL IN TABERNACLE
REV. SAM P. JONES AND REV. GEORGE STEWART TO
CONDUCT THE SERVICE

SKETCH OF REMARKABLE MAN

Capt. Thomas Green Ryman, probably the most widely known steamboat man and philanthropist south of the Ohio River, died yesterday afternoon at 3:45 o'clock, after an illness of two years. It has only been for the last three days that he was unconscious, but for some time before that he had not been able to leave an invalid chair.

He was at the time of his death surrounded by his wife, seven children, three sisters and one brother and several of his most intimate friends.

The funeral will take place Sunday afternoon at 2:30 o'clock, at the Union Gospel Tabernacle, and the services will be conducted by Revs. Sam P. Jones and George Stewart. It is probable that the great revival singer, E. O. Excell, will be here to lead the singing.

The Tabernacle trustees, the steamboat fraternity and Capt. R. V. Wright have been asked to act as honorary pallbearers, while the following gentlemen who had been very closely associated with the deceased during his lifetime, will serve in an active capacity: Capt. T. M. Gallagher, Capt. J. S. Tyner, William Culbert, H. W. Buttorff, J. B. Richardson, Robert M. Dudley and J. S. Dunbar. The ministers of the city have been requested to occupy seats on the platform.

The news of Capt. Ryman's death has caused unusual sorrow in this city, for no man had impressed his personality more upon the community at large than he. A shrewd business man, active and energetic, he was devoted to his friends, and of such staunch integrity that no personal consideration could swerve him a hair's breath from what he conceived to be his duty. With all the iron in his frame he was in nature as simple as a child, as gentle as a woman and generous in every impulse. The eyes of

68

many who have felt his kindness will be wet with tears today, and many a simple prayer will be offered in his behalf.

RYMAN AUDITORIUM

Five years ago Dr. Ira Landrith, in a card to the *Banner*, suggested that the name of the Gospel Tabernacle be changed to the Ryman Auditorium, as a mark of respect to Capt. Thomas G. Ryman, through whose untiring efforts this magnificent structure was erected. It has been suggested, now that Capt. Ryman is dead, that something should be done to perpetuate his name and that Nashville certainly owes him some marked recognition, and this could not be given in a more appropriate manner than to change the name of the Tabernacle to Ryman Auditorium, and let it stand as a lasting monument to the man who did so much for the material welfare of this city.

SKETCH OF LIFE

Capt. Ryman was born on October 12, 1841, and has been interested in river industries most of his life. His father was a river man before him and the deceased was associated with his father in business from the age of twelve or fourteen years—in fact at the age of fifteen he was practically the manager of the business. His career was begun at Chattanooga and it was near there that he managed the fishing business and shipped his catches to Nashville, where they were sold by his father. He went to Decatur near the beginning of the Civil War and after about a year's residence came to Nashville and from here went to Fort Henry. He fished for some time at the latter place, sending the fish across to Fort Donelson, where they were sold to the soldiers. After the fall of Fort Henry he came back to Nashville and entered school which he attended for a short while.

After he quit school in the year 1864, he went into business for himself and had associated with him Capt. J. S. Tyner, whom he had formerly employed at Chattanooga. Two fishing boats were procured and young Ryman went to Andrew Johnson, who at that time was the military Governor of Tennessee, and procured a permit to have his boats towed up the Tennessee River as far as Johnsonville by the United States gunboats. During the trip one of the fishing boats was sunk and partly demolished. Some of the nets were recovered, but the craft could not be

Northeastern view of monument on Ryman Lot, Mount Olivet Cemetery. The carving of the fishing boat and net symbolizes his early life as a fisherman, and his later life as a "fisher of men" for Christ.

used again. Johnsonville, which at that time was a base of supplies for the Federal forces, was reached with one boat, and after a short time of very successful fishing, this was burned with the rest of the boats at the wharf at the time the town was shelled by General Forrest. After this he had another boat built immediately at New Liberty, bought three more and began business on a larger scale than ever. Capt. Tyner was left in charge of two boats at Johnsonville while Capt. Ryman managed the work of the other two at Decatur.

The fishing business was finally abandoned after Capt. Ryman had saved quite a large amount of money at the business, and in 1865 he bought his first steamboat—the *Alpha*—for which he paid about $3,500 at New Orleans. The boat was brought to Nashville by his uncle, Capt. Charlie Ryman, as Capt. Ryman did not at that time have a master's license.

Since the days of the *Alpha*, Capt. Ryman has built and owned over thirty-five steamboats. The second was the *Eddyville*, which was built at Evansville, the machinery of his first boat being used. Probably the largest boat owned was the *Shipper's Own*, which was built at Brownsville, Pennsylvania. The majority of the other boats were built at Jeffersonville, Indiana.

Most Successful

Capt. Ryman was conceded to be one of the most successful, if he did not stand first, among the steamboat men of the South and West. He has been well and favorably known from Pittsburgh, on the Ohio, to St. Paul and New Orleans, on the Mississippi. In the operation of a boat he had about the best judgment of any man on the rivers on which his boats plied, when there was a wreck, especially, he knew exactly what should be done. Up until a few years ago, when his health failed, he was actively engaged in managing his business. Capt. Ryman has owned more boats than any other man ever doing business on the Cumberland River. . . .

Capt. Ryman had always been one of the most charitable of men and it was seldom a petition for aid was turned down.

There has been an idea prevalent that before his conversion at the meeting by Sam Jones, Capt. Ryman was a drinking man and was in fact a bad character. Several men with whom he has been intimately associated ever since his residence in Nashville were interviewed this morning by a *Banner* reporter and as a unit they expressed the opinion that he had never in his life taken a drink over a bar, and that he had never, to their certain knowledge, been drunk. This statement is made to correct a general impression, which has been probably caused by the fact that he was very often engaged in furthering the political aspirations of his friends and the fact that he was engaged very actively in politics at nearly all elections.

Converted Under Sam Jones

After his conversion by Sam Jones in a tent erected at the corner of Spruce and Broad streets during the first visit of the great evangelist to this city, Capt. Ryman conceived the idea of building a tabernacle in which he hoped to unite all denominations in bonds of brotherly love. He did not wish to alienate them from their different beliefs, but simply to unite them into a brotherhood for the furtherance of the Christian religion.

He, with the untiring energy which was one of his characteristics, began work along this line and the outcome has been the magnificent Tabernacle on Summer street which has come to be so appreciated by the people of this city. He was probably the largest contributor in money to its construction, and he was certainly the moving spirit in promoting the idea.

After Capt. Ryman had been converted, the leases for the bar privileges on his various boats were taken up as they expired, and he has not permitted one to be run on one of his boats since. An idea has become prevalent that he poured many barrels of whisky into the river at this time, but this story is without foundation. The discontinuing of the bars on his boats, of course, caused considerable loss of revenue, not only from the leases, but there is no doubt that traffic was considerably curtailed, for, as an old river man said to a *Banner* reporter, a well-conducted bar is often the life of a boat and attracts many who would otherwise prefer a more rapid means of transportation.

Sam Jones revival team and musicians socialize at Ryman home before services. Tom Ryman is second and Sam Jones is third from the left on the back row. Mrs. Jones and daughter are seated on the left of the bench and Bettie Ryman on the right.

Major Stahlman, vice president of the Tabernacle Association, has called a meeting of the trustees of the Tabernacle and subscribers to the Tabernacle fund to convene at the rooms of the Retail Merchants' Association at 3:30 this afternoon to take suitable action, which will be in the nature of appropriate resolutions on the life and character of Capt. Ryman, the sending of a floral tribute, arrangements to have the trustees of the Tabernacle attend the funeral in a body and such other proceedings as the intimate relations of the deceased with the Tabernacle and other laudable enterprises of the city may suggest.

A special meeting of the Retail Merchants' Association will be held this afternoon at 4 o'clock to take action on Capt. Ryman's death.

Causes Much Grief

COMMERCIAL BODIES TAKE ACTION ON DEATH OF
    CAPT. RYMAN
TABERNACLE TRUSTEES MEET

Following the announcement of the death of Capt. Thomas G. Ryman, which occurred at his residence on South Market Street on Friday afternoon, there was much sorrow throughout the city. Capt. Ryman has been closely identified with the business interest of Nashville, and his loss will be deeply felt. There were called meetings on Saturday of both the commercial organizations and the Board of Trustees of the Union Tabernacle, when action was then taken on his death.

The funeral of Capt. Ryman will take place this afternoon at 2:30 at the Tabernacle, of which splendid building Capt. Ryman was the founder and which will be an enduring monument to his life work. The services will be conducted by the Revs. Sam Jones and George Stewart, the noted evangelists, warm personal friends of Capt. Ryman. The original ushers at the Tabernacle at the time of its completion will serve this afternoon.

CHAMBER OF COMMERCE MEETS

Pres. H. W. Buttorff presided at the meeting of the Chamber of Commerce, and after calling the body to order stated that he had called the meeting to take action on the death of one of Nashville's most prominent and useful men. J. B. Richardson, Maj. E. B. Stahlman, Houston Dudley, P. M. Estes and others paid high tributes to Capt. Ryman. A committee on resolutions reported the following which was adopted:

> The announcement of the death of Capt. T. G. Ryman yesterday afternoon sent a pang of sorrow to every heart in our city, for he was universally known and beloved.
>
> For half a century he has occupied a prominent place in the commercial affairs of this community, and in that time his name has been linked with everything that tended to the good of our city or to benefit his fellowman.

He was born in Nashville, where nearly all his life has been spent, started with no capital save energy, honesty and unimpeachable integrity and acquired success beyond that of the average man.

He was genial, generous, gentle, charitable and just, and his life was a blessing to all who knew him. We thank God that he was permitted to live until his life was fully rounded up, that it might be seen in all its phases, and men made better for having seen it.

We recommend his life to our young men as most worthy of emulation, and assure them if they will take it as their guide and live up to it, they will not only be useful in this world, but better still, will be prepared, like he was for the summons, however sudden.

Resolved, that in Capt. Ryman's death Nashville loses one of its best and most exemplary citizens; the poor and needy one of their best friends, and his family sustains a loss that is irreparable, for there never lived a better husband or father. To his bereaved family we extend our sincere sympathies and commend them to that God who has so tenderly cared for their husband and father during his long and useful life.

Resolved, that a copy of these resolutions be spread upon the minutes of this organization, a copy furnished to the family of our deceased friend, and a copy to the press.

(Signed) Leland Hume, Chairman;

Houston Dudley,

L. Jonas,

W. G. Hirsig,

J. B. Richardson.

RETAIL MERCHANTS

There was a meeting of the Retail Merchants' Association to take action on the death of Capt. Ryman at 4 on Saturday afternoon, in accordance with a call of the President, Charles F. Frizzell. Mr. Frizzell, after calling the meeting to order, referred to the purpose and to the great loss in the death of Capt. Ryman. A committee on resolutions was appointed and $25 was appropriated for decorations at the Tabernacle. The committee reported the following resolutions, which were adopted:

Resolved, that we have learned with profound sorrow of the death of Capt. Thomas G. Ryman, for so many years identified with all that was for the best interests of the City of Nashville.

He was honest, upright and consistent in all things that he considered right and has therefore in his life set us a worthy example for our emulation. No one needy, however poor or humble, who came within the sphere of his influence but were benefited thereby. In the erection and completion of the Union Tabernacle, his most earnest desire for the unification of all creeds was realized.

Be it further resolved, that in the death of Capt. Ryman the City of Nashville has lost a good man and a useful citizen; that we bow to the Divine will with meekness and humility.

Be it further resolved, that these resolutions be spread upon the minutes of this association, and that a copy be sent to the family of the deceased.

(Signed) Joseph Frank,
E. B. Stahlman,
George R. Knox,
Dr. R. B. Lees,
R. J. McKay.

TABERNACLE TRUSTEES

There was a meeting at 3 on Saturday afternoon of the Board of Trustees of the Union Tabernacle for the purpose of taking action on the death of Capt. Ryman. The meeting was called to order by Maj. E. B. Stahlman, who stated that a leader in a great work had been lost in the death of Capt. Ryman, and that the board had been called together.

It was moved and seconded that a committee of five be appointed to draft resolutions on the death of Capt. Ryman. Maj. Stahlman appointed Capt. T. M. Steger, Rev. I. Lewinthal, George R. Knox, L. Jonas and R. L. Dudley.

The Board of Trustees will meet at the Retail Merchants' Association at 1:45 this afternoon to attend the funeral of Capt. Ryman in a body. Carriages for the Trustees will leave promptly at the time mentioned.

The original ushers of the Tabernacle were requested to serve at the funeral and to report to Mr. Whitehall at the Tabernacle at 1:30 this afternoon.

A motion to decorate the Tabernacle prevailed, and the decorations will remain in the building for thirty days. The chair appointed Joseph Frank, C. T. Cheek and J. H. DeWitt a committee to arrange the decorations.

J. B. Richardson, Edgar Jones and L. Jonas were appointed a committee to report on a memorial to Capt. Ryman. The committee was instructed to report at some future meeting of the Board of Trustees.

Capt. T. G. Ryman

FUNERAL SERVICE IS HELD FOR HIM AT TABERNACLE WITH 4,000 PERSONS PRESENT

Rare are the times in Nashville when scenes more beautifully impressive or more solemnly pathetic have been enacted or witnessed on the Sabbath Christmas afternoon than at the Tabernacle when thousands of persons gathered at the funeral services for Capt. Thomas G. Ryman, to pay a last sad, loving tribute to his memory. It was such a gathering, such a service as fitted the ending of such a life.

Evangelists whose names are measured in recognition only by the limits of the Nation came to mingle their tears and sympathy with the bereaved ones of this family. Men who stand for the strength and greatness of Nashville, and women who honored the purity and stead-fastness of his life, joined in doing homage to this truly good man's memory, and showed by their presence and emotion that, in his passing, they had sustained a personal loss. And yet none the less impressive and beautiful was the mute but eloquent expression of love from those of the simpler, humbler walks. He had been their friend in silence and without ostentation, and they thronged the place to listen with tear-dimmed eyes to the words of beautiful truth said of this golden-hearted man.

DEEP FEELING DISPLAYED

Such feeling as was displayed at the funeral service for Capt. Ryman must stand as a monument to his memory, grander and more enduring than marble or brass. Grief-stricken hearts they were that spoke, natures that were bowed beneath a burden of heaviest sorrow. People they were who had known him as he was day after day, who had profited by his friendship, who had been strengthened by his counsel, who had been made better for his having lived.

The funeral service for Capt. Ryman would have been a time for tears and sorrow on any day and in any season. But there was more of sadness, more of pathos in the performance of the last solemn rites on a day commemorative of the hour when, from the manger of Bethlehem and over the Judean hills, the world received its message of peace and joy and goodwill. Homes were saddened on Christmas Day in the knowledge that Capt. Ryman was dead and hearts were bowed in heavy submissiveness. But from the words that were said of him, words that made tears spring from the heart, the thousands who knew and loved him were comforted in the knowledge of the reward that is his.

Probably no higher tribute to Capt. Ryman's memory could have been paid than the eagerness with which the suggestion of Rev. Sam P. Jones was received to have the Union Gospel Tabernacle to be known henceforth as the Ryman Auditorium. Nothing need be told of what Capt. Ryman and Mr. Jones did toward the establishment of the Tabernacle. It was at the close of his remarks that Mr. Jones offered the suggestion. He referred to Capt. Ryman's love for the Tabernacle and his interest in it. He said that it would be appropriate for it to be known now as the Ryman Auditorium, and that a marble slab as pure as Capt. Ryman's own life would be put upon the building's walls, to be seen in future years by those who come and go. He then asked all who desired to have this name given to the building to rise, and as one person the thousands who heard him were upon their feet.

More than 4,000 persons gathered in the Tabernacle on Sunday afternoon at this solemn services. For an hour and a half before the appointed hour for the service the streams of humanity from every direction poured into the place. Every age, every class and condition of society was represented, from wealth to poverty, from position to simplicity. Steadily the number increased until, when the service was started at 3:35, almost every seat held an occupant, while many stood near the stage that they might the better see and hear.

Tabernacle in Mourning

Both inside and out the Tabernacle had been appropriately draped for the occasion. Over the entrance streamed the solemn drapings of black and white, while beneath were twined flags of the Nation. The entire balcony rail was covered with the mourning hues with National flags

Extreme Funeral

below, while each post was wrapped with bunting of the colors of the Union. The stage was covered with palms and ferns and other foliage, which offered background for the myriad and magnificent floral tributes which had been sent almost without number. There were 100 chairs upon the stage, all of which were occupied, and upon the back wall over the heads of all were spread the folds of the Stars and Stripes.

The funeral procession entered the Tabernacle a few minutes after the appointed time. First came Dr. Felix Hill, who read the processional. Next were Rev. Sam P. Jones, of Cartersville, Georgia, and Rev. George Stewart, of Cleveland, Tennessee, the two world-famous evangelists, whose lives had been closely linked with that of Capt. Ryman, and who came to offer by their words a departing tribute to his worth and his memory.

The honorary escort followed, made up of the Tabernacle trustees and other prominent men with whom Capt. Ryman had been associated. After them was borne the casket, the pallbearers being Capt. T. M. Gallagher, Capt. J. S. Tyner, William Culbert, H. W. Buttorff, J. B. Richardson, Robert M. Dudley and J. S. Dunbar. The members of the immediate family and their friends followed in the solemn procession. The casket was placed at the foot of the stage, the members of the immediate family occupying seats nearest there, reserved for them. As the procession moved into the Tabernacle the beautiful hymn, "Must Jesus Bear the Cross Alone?" was sung by the quartet upon the stage. This was composed of Miss Lillie Wooton, soprano; Miss Etta Nimmerfall, contralto; A. B. Armstrong, tenor; W. W. Knox, basso, and Guy McCullom, accompanist.

Seats were reserved upon the stage for the members of Mrs. Ryman's Sunday School class, and were occupied by them without a member missing. Upon the stage with Revs. Jones, Stewart and Hill were Elder Moore, Dr. W. M. Anderson, R. W. Turner, Alex Perry, Capt. T. M. Steger, J. P. Thornley, Mayor A. S. Williams, Dr. W. J. McMurray, S. A. Cunningham, Rev. John B. McFerrin, Rev. T. C. Ragsdale, Maj. John W. Thomas and Dr. J. M. Frost, Dr. W. F. Tillett, Prof. O. E. Brown, Rev. J. R. Stewart, Rev. J. L. Brownlee, Maj. E. B. Stahlman, Joseph Frank, W. E. Norvell and Dr. W. T. Haggard.

Near the stage were 60 of the river men who for years had worked for Capt. Ryman. As their employer, as their friend and as a man they had learned to know him, to love and honor him, and among the thousands in that gathering there were none more visibly affected than they.

Mr. Jones' Eloquence

An opening prayer was offered by Rev. Felix Hill and after the singing of "Lead, Kindly Light," Mr. Jones stepped to the front of the stage. It was a moment before he could speak, for he was deeply affected. Then, as a silence that one could almost feel came over the place, Mr. Jones spoke. With his simplicity but earnestness of style, Mr. Jones' words went straight to the hearts of his hearers, and almost during the entire time heads were bared and sobs were heard to come from every part of that vast throng.

"Occasions like this are rare in Nashville," said Mr. Jones. "They are rare everywhere. A more representative audience never gathered in Nashville than fills this Tabernacle this afternoon. There is not a life in this city from the highest to the lowest that the life of Capt. Ryman did not touch. It is fitting on a Christmas day, on a Sabbath Christmas day that we should meet to mingle our sympathy, our tears and our love.

"I go into the garden of my own heart and pluck the rarest and sweetest flowers that ever blossomed there, and lay them on his grave. I go into the deepest garden of my thoughts and take from there the best it ever held, to give it to the memory of Tom Ryman. Thank God for the privilege of speaking a word and offering testimony for him. It will take 50 years of measurement and calculation for Nashville to realize what Tom Ryman was to this city. Statesmen and warriors have their marble slabs and memorials erected to them, but Nashville piles thousands of hearts together in sympathy and love for this noble man."

Mr. Jones then spoke of the presence there of Rev. George Stewart, who loved and was loved by Capt. Ryman, stating that Mr. Stewart would be heard and that he would then offer a word in conclusion.

Mr. Stewart's Tribute

Beautifully and eloquently did Mr. Stewart pay his tribute to the life of Capt. Ryman. He said when the telephone call came to his home that Capt. Ryman was dead he answered that he would be here Sunday to stand beside the coffin and speak from his heart. He said that when wife and children asked him if he would be absent from them on Christmas Day he answered, "Tom Ryman is dead and I must go. To no other place would I go at this time, but I shall be there." He spoke of the simple, pure character of Capt. Ryman and his humble but unfaltering faith in God.

"We are here to pay our tribute of love," he said, "to one whom so many loved, not as an orator, not as a man of letters, but a man of something higher than all this, an humble child of Jesus Christ. He was a Christian as were few men I have ever known. 'Blessed are the poor in spirit,' if there ever was a humble man, who made no flourish, but in all humility, put his Savior before all else, that man was Capt. Tom Ryman.

"Everybody trusted him. There was never a word or thought of impeachment of anything he ever said or did, for his word was his bond. His faith in God was beautiful. I never knew a man whose simple, earnest, childlike faith took such a hold upon the Master."

Mr. Stewart then referred to incidents in the life of Capt. Ryman, where he had brought others to Christ, saying he was a man who spoke, not with words but with his heart. Humbly and with heart and steadfast faith, he said, Capt. Ryman was always working for others.

"A city never gets over the fact," he continued, "of a great man living so humbly, one whose great spirit has been exalted to that blessed home. I say with Brother Jones that I lay the sweetest and the rarest flowers of my heart upon this great man's grave."

His Life an Example

"His life is an example to every one to be better. His life is an example to every Christian man and woman to do more for God. He labored quietly but faithfully, and God's crown has come to him at last. To his family his life will be a beacon light to guide them home. May his memory be a balm of consolation to lead us all to the life he loved."

Following the conclusion of Mr. Stewart's remarks, Mr. Jones spoke briefly in conclusion:

"It was just 21 years ago," he said, "under a canvas tent on Broad Street, a man who I did not know came to the altar for prayer. That man was Tom Ryman, and from that time until the end he was a changed man, a new man, a Christian man. In my travels over forty odd States and in Canada, I want to say that I have never met a Tom Ryman anywhere. God makes few of them. That which charmed one in him was his pure transparency of character. The crystal river of life that flows from the great white throne, was no more pure or clear than the life of Tom Ryman.

"There was no hypocrisy or makeshift about him. Whatever he said, he meant. He was so royal and Christian like that he charmed you as few men can. The more I looked at Tom Ryman the bigger he got and smaller grew the infidel."

Mr. Jones spoke of the awful effect of infidelism upon the gospel and how Capt. Ryman's life was a burning rebuke to that belief.

"Tom Ryman was a simple-hearted man," he continued. "He was like a child in his faith, and I want to tell you, the more you become like a child, the better you please God. The simplicity of his heart, the truthfulness of his nature, the transparency of his character, all were like unto a little child. Thank God for a man like Tom Ryman. A purer, stronger, nobler man, truer to God than he, I have never met."

Speaker Is Affected

At this point Mr. Jones' voice failed him as he choked, and, with tears in his eyes, was compelled to pause for a moment.

"To his widow and his children," he continued a moment later, "I have spoken from the fullness of a heart of grief and sympathy. If there is an uncrowned queen on earth, it is his widow. God bless them all, and may Tom Ryman stand at the gates of pearl some day and see the last one come in. He will be there."

It was then that Mr. Jones made the suggestion relative to changing the name of the Tabernacle to Ryman Auditorium. Prayer was offered by Elder Moore. Following this the quartet sang, "Asleep in Jesus," while the casket was taken from the Tabernacle, the procession following. From the Tabernacle the course led to Mount Olivet Cemetery, the place of burial of the remains.

Nashville American, *December 24, 1904 Editorial*
Thomas G. Ryman

Thomas G. Ryman, the aged steamboatman who lies dead at his home in this city, leaves as a heritage to his children a name which is better than riches. He was not an educated man because he never had time, as boy, youth or man, to acquire education. Always busy, always seeking to promote those interests dearest to his heart, he had no time for leisure. No more charitable man ever lived in Nashville. His charity was unostentatious, it was real, and it will abide in the hearts of those whose benefactor he had been. A man of the strictest integrity, his word was his bond. No man needed any other, no matter what was involved. He was the Father of the Tabernacle. It is his monument, and while he has perished, that splendid auditorium will abide to often remind those who visit it of the charitable and deeply religious man whose efforts gave it to Nashville.

Nashville Banner, *Saturday evening, December 24, 1904, Editorial*

CAPT. THOMAS G. RYMAN
Capt. Thomas G. Ryman was a noteworthy citizen of Nashville whose death will be generally regretted. Born in the city, the greater part of his life was identified with Nashville and especially with the steamboat business on the Cumberland. No man was better known in the city and his career was one that brought him into contact with a great number of people. With very little education, he had the aggressive and persistent qualities that enabled him to achieve success, and eventually to earn for himself recognition as a public benefactor. He was a man of firm convictions, with an unfaltering courage to maintain them. Much of

his life was the rough life of a river man, and for years he was a conspicuous exponent of that life in its demands for self-assertion and in its vicissitudes of exposure and experience. In his later years he gave more time and thought to matters of public interest and was the projector and the main promoter of the Union Gospel Tabernacle, which as a great auditorium is an acknowledged public benefaction. It was when Capt. Ryman became a professed Christian that he conceived the idea of the Tabernacle, to the erection of which he was a most generous contributor. The Tabernacle became his pet idea, and very largely through his instrumentality and persistent labor, often under many discouragements, the building was completed and stands today admittedly a monument to his memory. Capt. Ryman was one of the best and most tenderhearted of men. He was quick to give relief to suffering and this community will never know the extent of his charities. He knew life in all its phases and he was easily touched by the appeals of sorrow or misfortune. As a Christian he took strong and sometimes, perhaps, strange grounds, and was true and consistent, making any sacrifice which he deeded necessary and never failed to stand by his convictions. He was a true and staunch friend. Nashville will long remember Capt. Tom Ryman.

Capt. Ryman's Career

To the Editor of the *American*: After returning from Nashville, where we were called on account of the serious illness and death of our brother, Capt. T. G. Ryman, through the kindness of some of our friends we received the papers in which articles appeared concerning the death of our brother and the description of his life as a business man and as a Christian worker.

All of them gave true accounts and kind words, which are highly appreciated, with the exception of one paragraph under the heading of "His Business Career," in your paper of December 24, in which you say:

"Capt. Ryman began his business life with his father in the steamboat business. Unfortunate investments financially ruined the elder Ryman, and he died penniless in 1864, leaving Capt. Ryman, then 23 years old, to support his mother, one brother and three sisters, to do which he set manfully to work. Although he directed his energies in humble channels, he kept the family together, weathering financial shoals and evidencing those sterling qualities and the business acumen which formed the foundations of his successes of later years."

That part of your article is positively incorrect, and it is a great injustice to Capt. Tom Ryman's father. It is true that Capt. John Ryman Sr. was unfortunate in some of his investments at one time, but he himself, with his business sagacity, his untiring energy and industry, kept his business intact, and accumulated considerable property. In fact, he gave young Tom Ryman his first start, and his younger brother, John Ryman Jr., worked energetically with his father and his brother.

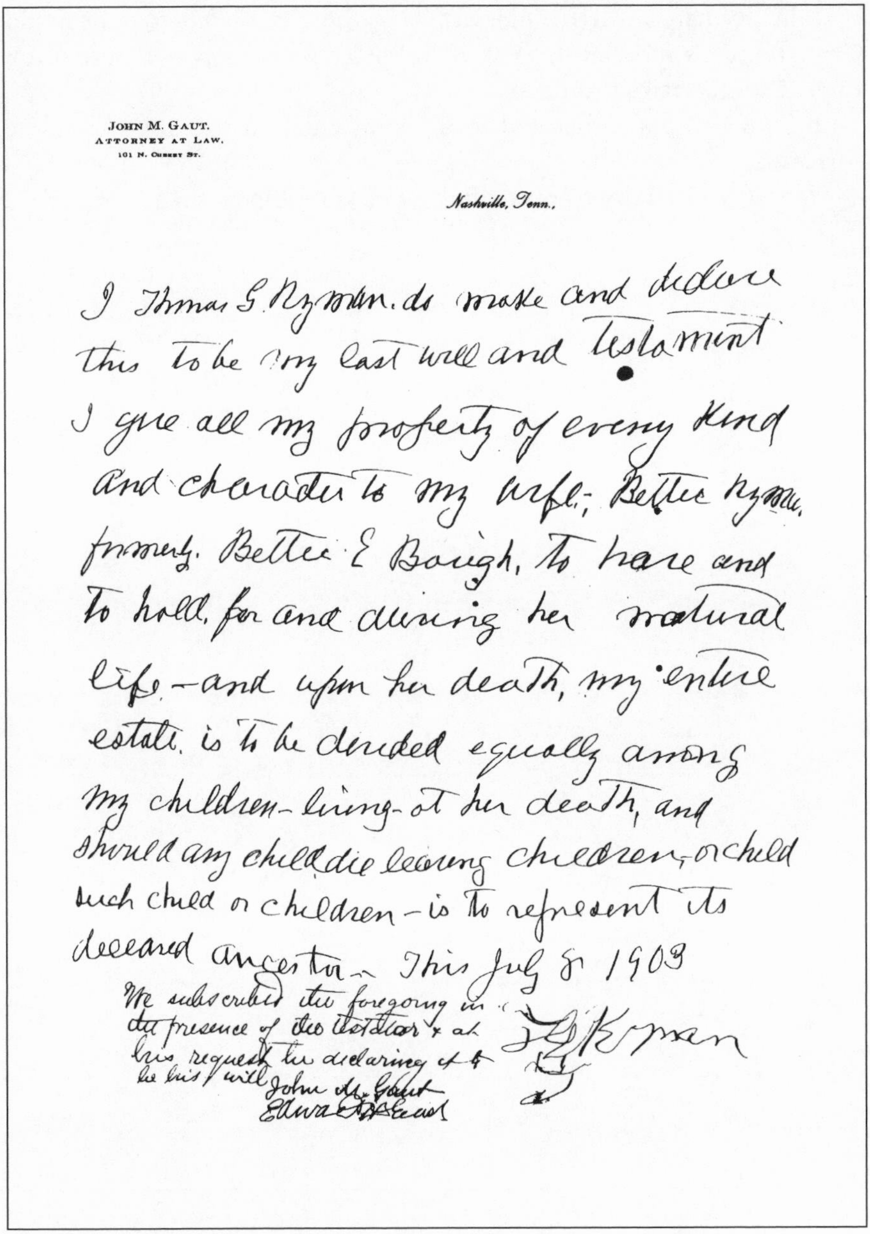

JOHN M. GAUT.
ATTORNEY AT LAW.
101 N. Cherry St.

Nashville, Tenn.,

I Thomas G Ryman. do make and declare this to be my last will and Testament I give all my property of every kind and character to my wife; Bettie Ryman, formerly Bettie E Baugh, To have and To hold, for and during her natural life — and upon her death, my entire estate. is to be devided equally among my children — living at her death, and should any child die leaving children, or child such child or children — is to represent its deceased ancestor — This July 8 1903

We subscribed the foregoing in the presence of the testator & at his request he declaring it to be his will John M. Gaut
Edward _____

T G Ryman

Last Will and Testament of Thomas Green Ryman. Courtesy of Metropolitan Government Archives.

John Ryman Sr., left a nice estate in the city of Chattanooga, and Capt. Ryman's mother, as well as his sisters, were never a burden on Capt. Tom Ryman's shoulders.

It is due to our father and to us as his children that this should be corrected.

We ask you kindly to make the proper corrections in your paper.

Respectfully,
Mrs. C. W. Biese,
Mrs. F. M. Carell,
Mrs. V. M. Moore,
Chattanooga, Tennessee

PART 5

FAMILY
CELEBRATIONS

Daisy Ryman and Gus Coggins

26

Mr. Gus Coggins left last Tuesday for Nashville, Tennessee, accompanied by his brothers, John, Charlie, and Raleigh, where on Wednesday evening at 7:30 o'clock he and Miss Daisy Ryman were united in marriage at the home of Capt. T. G. Ryman, the bride's father, by Rev. Mr. Cave. The happy couple are now enjoying a visit to points of interest in Florida after which they will return to Canton and, as soon as the workmen can turn over the keys, will occupy their beautiful dwelling and be "at home" to their many friends. The groom is Cherokee's popular sheriff and one of the county's big-hearted and most noble, whole-souled young men, a good business man and upright, honorable gentleman; while the bride is a beautiful and accomplished young lady with a large circle of friends and the daughter of Capt. T. G. Ryman, one of the leading businessmen in Nashville. The bride has some acquaintances in Canton which she formed while on a visit here a few years ago to Miss Ada Jordan with whom she attended the Peabody Normal College in Nashville. The hearty good wishes and congratulations of all our readers are tendered Mr. and Mrs. Coggins. May all the best things of this life be theirs.

Pearl Ryman and Roll Coggins

At 8 o'clock p.m. on Wednesday of next week a marriage will be solemnized at 514 So. Market St., Nashville, TN., in which Canton feels much interest and which will make marital honors again easy between Georgia and Tennessee. In the above recited marriage the State of Georgia will be receiving one of Tennessee's loveliest brides, the groom also being a fortunate winner, justly happy in his choice. We refer, of course, to the marriage of Miss Pearl Ryman, daughter of Capt. T. G. Ryman of Nashville to Mr. Roll Coggins of this place. Immediately after the ceremony that makes the twain one is pronounced by Rev. Linn Cave, of the Christian church, Mr. and Mrs. Coggins will leave for Canton, reaching here the following morning. They will go at once to Mr. and Mrs. Gus Coggins' lovely home near town where rooms have been furnished for them, Mrs. Gus Coggins being a sister of Miss Ryman. Mr. Coggins is one of Canton's most popular young men while the bride is a beautiful young woman of lovable character. The *Advance* and its many friends extend congratulations and best wishes in advance to this happy event.

Louise Ryman and James Crozier Buchanan

The marriage of Miss Louise Ryman and James Buchanan last night at 6:30 o'clock at the home of the bride's parents, Capt. and Mrs. Thomas G. Ryman, was celebrated in the presence of a hundred and fifty guests, assembled to participate in the happiness of this popular couple. The wedding arrangements were effective in their simplicity. The ceremony was performed in the double parlors, which had decorations of palm plants. There were no attendants, the bride and groom entering together and standing during the saying of the ceremony on a large white rug spread between the double doors.[1] Miss Foster Jones, at the piano, rendered Mendelsohn's wedding march, and, as the wedding vows were spoken, the Cavaleria Rusticana intermezzo. A pretty bit of sentiment lay in the fact that the officiating minister, Rev. E. G. Sewell, also performed the marriage ceremony of the bride's parents. He was assisted on this occasion by Rev. J. Bunyan Stephens.

Miss Ryman was gowned in heavy white taffeta silk, trimmed in ruffles of white chiffon and an applique of seed pearls. A flower garniture of orange blossoms was on the corsage, and a bunch of the same flowers fastened the long veil of tulle in place. The bridal bouquet was a chatelaine of bride roses and Roman hyacinths.

The bride was never lovelier than when she spoke the marriage vows that bound her to the sweetheart of her school days.

Mr. Buchanan is the second son of Mr. and Mrs. Edward Buchanan. He is connected with J. H. Fall & Company.

Following the ceremony the wedding cake was cut, and the guests signed a wedding register, kept by Miss Fanny Hill. At 7 o'clock the bride and groom left for a wedding trip on the boat *Dunbar* to Burnside,

Mrs. Ryman and friends in the snow, February 11, 1901. When the Ryman daughters and friends got together to decorate and prepare for Dot and James's wedding, Bettie Ryman (standing on the porch) surprised them by having a photographer come and take a picture to give them as a keepsake of the happy occasion.

Kentucky. After their return they will reside with the groom's grand parents, Mr. & Mrs. William Culbert, on Rutledge Hill.

The bride's going away gown was a black-made gown trimmed with turquoise cloth and gold braid.

Dot's Wedding

by Mrs. Alabama Rountree

February 12, 1901—A little after six when we descended some of the guests had arrived, we registered and then took in the presents which were numerous and beautiful. Every minute brought new guests, so I got hold of Sister [Bettie Ryman] and went into Dot's [Louise Ryman's] room. She had just gotten from under the hairdryer. We all took part in dressing her and she was so beautiful and sweet. She was the happiest bride I ever saw, there was not a shadow about her, not even a serious look. She would break out into snatches of songs and trills and was just bubbling over with happiness all the time we were dressing her. She was so happy it affected everyone around her, the strained look on Sister's face changed to a cheerful satisfied one, and no one else had the heart to be sad when she seemed to happy. James passed through the room to get into your papa's room. Dot says, "James, are you scared?" "No, are you?" "Not a bit." After he shut the door they kept up a continual running conversation, neither one seemed the least embarrassed. They seemed more like two children bent on having a good time. When they were about ready Sister told me to tell Bro. Sewell where to stand. I went in the sitting room and found your papa entertaining him by showing him the pictures of his grandchildren.[1]

Leslie Ryman and Walter Franklin Barton

BARTON—RYMAN

The marriage of Miss Leslie Ryman and Mr. Walter Franklin Barton of Atlanta took place Tuesday evening at the residence of the bride's parents, Capt. and Mrs. Thomas Ryman, on South Market Street in the presence of a large assemblage of friends. Throughout the house clusters of snowballs, calla lilies, carnations, and other white flowers were arranged with grouped palms. The ceremony took place in an alcove in the first of the double parlors, where a curtain of green vines caught with white satin bows and a suspended white floral bell with a flower clapper were most effective. The ceremony was performed by Elder E. G. Sewell, who officiated at the marriage of the bride's mother and father, assisted by the Rev. C. A. Moore, her pastor. The Italian orchestra played the wedding music.

The bridal party was led by two little ribbon-bearers, Miss Louise Aul and Master Lee Rol Coggins, who wore dainty white costumes. These were followed by the ten bridesmaids and the two matrons of honor, who were Misses Eddie Barton and Annie May Harding of Atlanta, Dora and Sue Warfield and Laura Ely of Clarksville, Nell Tyner, Annette and Fannie Hill and Lula and Fannie Griffin, Mrs. James C. Buchanan and Mrs. T. Rol Coggins of Atlanta, all of whom wore white organdy gowns with sashes of green panne satin and carried clusters of white carnations. The maid of honor, Miss Georgia Ryman, entered alone, preceding the bride and wearing a gown of white organdy and lace with pink panne satin ribbons and a bouquet of pink roses. The bride was beautiful in a gown of white taffeta finished with a bertha and flounce of duchens lace in a snowball design, with a yoke of shirred chiffon. Her tulle veil was caught with pearl pins and her chattelaine bouquet was of bride roses. Mr. Barton was attended by Mr. D. C. Simms of Atlanta as best man.

Mr. and Mrs. Barton left last night for Atlanta, where they will reside at College Park, the bride being attired in a going away gown of dark, blue taffeta with a hat to match and a pongee cloak. Many handsome wedding gifts were received, including mahogany furniture from the bride's parents. Among the guests from a distance who attended the wedding were Mrs. V. M. Moore, Mrs. C. W. Biese and Mrs. F. M. Carell of Chattanooga.

Paul Milton Ryman and Lera Fletcher Sims

RYMAN—SIMS

A wedding which, by reason of a recent family bereavement was quietly solemnized, was that of Miss Lera Fletcher Sims and Mr. Paul Milton Ryman; which took place at 6:30 o'clock last night at the home of the bride's mother, Mrs. James Sims, on Russell and Thirteenth Streets. Rev. G. W. Shelton was the officiant, and an interested assemblage of sixty relatives and near friends were in attendance. An altar of palms, vines and flowers marked the place for the ceremony, the decorations of bouquets of pink carnations, ferns and smilax being continued throughout the house.

The bride made a charming picture in a Parisian gown of pale pink crepe de chene [*sic*] and rose pointe lace, with rosettes of green chiffon. She carried a bouquet of bride roses. The wedding music was played by Miss Nannie Lu Joseph, and there were no attendants.

Mrs. Sims, the bride's mother, who was gowned in a black voile and silk, with touches of jet, was assisted in receiving by Mrs. Harry Wand, who wore champagne voile, and Miss Lena Davis, whose reception costume was of lavender crepe de chene [*sic*]. A delightful bridal menu was served. The table had a floral centerpiece of pink carnations, and ferns, and streamers of green and white ribbon radiated from the chandelier to the table rim. From silver services Miss Katherine Sims and Susie Gilbert poured coffee and chocolate. The ices were heart-shaped, and the individual cakes simulated bride roses.

After a ten-days' trip East Mr. and Mrs. Ryman will return to Nashville and make their home with the latter's mother. The bride's going-away gown was a brown tailored cloth, with a silk blouse to match and mink toque and furs. Among the wedding guests from a distance were Mrs. M. C. Pruett of Chattanooga, Dr. and Mrs. J. H. White of Bell Buckle, Mr. William Livingstone of Memphis, and Mr. and Mrs. Gus Coggins of Canton, Ga.

Many valuable wedding gifts were received by the young people, including a silver service from the bride's mother, a chest of silver from her brothers, Dr. W. F. Sims and Messrs. Roy and James Sims, with handsome silver from the groom's family.

Georgia Ryman and William Edwin Jackson

JACKSON-RYMAN

A company of relatives and intimate friends witnessed the marriage of Miss Georgia Ryman to William Edwin Jackson Thursday evening at 8 o'clock, at the residence of the bride's mother, Mrs. Thomas G. Ryman, on Second Avenue South. The bride is the youngest daughter of the lamented Thomas G. Ryman. On account of his recent death [Dec. 23, 1904] all the wedding arrangements were made as simple as possible, and the usual reception for congratulations was omitted after the ceremony, and the bride and groom left at once for a southern trip.

The bride laid aside her mourning for the wedding costume, and chose for that occasion a charming toilet of white embroidered over taffeta and chiffon, and finished with frills of real lace. Her veil of tule was put on with a diamond pin, given by the groom, and her flowers were bride roses made into a chatelaine.

Mrs. James Buchanan, the bride's sister, served as matron of honor, and she and the bridesmaids, Misses Lulu and Fannie Griffin and Miss Annette Hill were gowned alike in white taffeta silk, with light blue girdles and slippers, and bouquets of La France roses. The bride was given in marriage by her brother, Paul Ryman. The groom's best man was H. T. Hill, and they were proceeded into the parlor by two pretty children, Miss Mary Louise Buchanan and Master Tom Coggins of Georgia. The four ribbon bearers were Misses Elizabeth Coggins and Margaret Tolmie, and Masters Robert Dudley and Lee Rol Coggins.

The ceremony was performed by Elder E. G. Sewell who officiated at the marriage of the bride's parents. Mrs. Ryman was assisted in receiving by Mrs. S. H. Orr, Mrs. H. H. Dudley Jr., Mrs. R. M. Dudley and Mrs. J. A. Rountree. The reception rooms were beautifully decorated. The ceremony took place before a curtain of wild smilax, and above the heads of the bride and groom hung a chatelaine of white carnations tied with a true lovers' knot of white tulle. Bouquets of white roses, lilies and carnations were about the room. In the library a collection of handsome wedding presents were displayed, among them being a handsome chest of silver from the groom's uncle, Robert Orr. On their return from the south they will make their home with the groom's sister, Mrs. Burton Donnan, on Woodland Street. Mrs. Jackson's going away gown was a black tailored suit with a hat to match.

PART 6

FAMILY
SORROWS

Nashville American, *Tuesday, April 2, 1912*

Mrs. Louise Ryman Buchanan

Mrs. Louise Ryman Buchanan, aged 31 years, died Monday afternoon at 1:15 o'clock at the residence of her mother, Mrs. T. G. Ryman, 514 Second Avenue, South. She was the wife of James C. Buchanan, and has been a resident of Nashville all her life.

Mrs. Buchanan possessed an unusually sweet and genial disposition and wherever she went the radiance of her happy spirit seemed to permeate the surroundings. She had been a member of the Third Avenue Christian Church for a number of years, having taught a Sunday school class of young ladies and gentlemen for some time. Every member of the class was devoted to her. Nowhere did her genial nature seem more evident than in her own home.

Mrs. Buchanan is survived by her husband, two children, a mother, four sisters, Mesdames Gus and Rol Coggins, and Walter Barton of Atlanta, and Edwin Jackson, of Nashville; two brothers, Tom and Paul Ryman, of Nashville.

Funeral services at the residence this afternoon (Tuesday) at 2 o'clock, by Rev. C. A. Moore. Interment at Mt. Olivet: private.

Following are the pallbearers: H. T. Hill, Paul Moore, W. H. Buchanan, F. S. Green, J. F. Fleming, R. B. C. Howell, D. A. Lipscomb and A. S. Coggins. Carriages from W. R. Cornelius & Co.

Nashville Banner, *Saturday Evening, July 31, 1915*

Tragedy on Cumberland

CAPT. THOS. G. RYMAN KILLED ON STEAMER
JO HORTON FALL
SHOT FOUR TIMES AND DIES INSTANTLY—
SLAYER IMMEDIATELY PLACED UNDER ARREST
MEN LONG UNFRIENDLY

Capt. Thomas G. Ryman of the steamer *Jo Horton Fall* was killed this morning at 7 o'clock on his boat near Hunter's Point, in Trousdale County, by Wilson Montgomery, a pilot. Capt. Ryman was one of the best known steamboat men in this section, being a son of the late Thomas G. Ryman, noted as a steamboat owner, and by whose efforts the construction of the Ryman Auditorium in this city was due.

Mr. Montgomery is a pilot by profession, but not employed at present. He lives near Hunter's Point, where the tragedy occurred. He got on the boat at Walker's Landing, near Hunter's Point, with his wife and two girls while Capt. Ryman was at breakfast.

It is said he had a conference with Capt. Ryman in a private apartment of the boat, and after they had come out seemingly desired to renew the conference. Shortly thereafter he called, "Oh, Cap" to Capt. Ryman, and the shooting began. The weapon used was an automatic pistol. Capt. Ryman was shot four times below the right nipple, under the left ear, severing the jugular vein, in the mouth and under the right ear. Capt. Ryman died instantly. The boat went on to Hartsville, where Montgomery was placed under arrest by Sheriff J. R. Parkhurst and Deputy H. A. Parkins.

The remains of Capt. Ryman were sent on the 10:20 train this morning from Hartsville to Nashville.

Montgomery appeared cool and collected after the killing, but would make no statement. It is said, however, that bad blood had existed between the two men for some time. It was said in Hartsville this morning that Mr. William Walker, Montgomery's father-in-law, who lived near Walker's Landing, owned a minority interest in the boat and recently bought a majority interest and that Montgomery's conference with Capt. Ryman this morning was due to the fact that he desired to obtain a position as pilot on the boat.

Montgomery is 20 years of age.

Capt. Ryman was 42 years old and leaves a wife and one son, Thomas G. Ryman III. They live in this city at 514 Second Avenue, South.

The news of the tragic death of Capt. Ryman was received by his brother, Paul Ryman, who is also connected with the Ryman Line, shortly after 8 o'clock this morning. He left for Hartsville in his automobile immediately.

Montgomery, the slayer, was formerly employed as pilot on the steamer *Jo Horton Fall*, having been discharged by Capt. Thomas Ryman a few months ago. Since that time Montgomery and Capt. Ryman had been on bad terms and had engaged in several heated quarrels according to local steamboat men. The information received by the officials of the Ryman Line here is that Montgomery left for Hartsville in an automobile yesterday afternoon.

The steamer *Jo Horton Fall* left Nashville at 5 o'clock Friday afternoon and was en route to West Point, Tenn. It reached Hartsville shortly after 7 o'clock this morning.

Montgomery's father-in-law, William Walker, it is said, had a difficulty with Capt. Ryman of the boat which resulted in a lawsuit a year ago. The slayer was employed to pilot the boat by his father-in-law and was discharged as the result of trouble with Capt. Ryman, it is said.

Mr. W. H. Buchanan, president of the Nashville Packet Company, when asked about the report that Mr. Walker had recently bought a majority interest in the *Jo Horton Fall*, said this was a mistake, but that he was a minority stockholder.

HELD WITHOUT BOND
Preliminary Trial of Montgomery for Ryman Murder

Hartsville, Tenn. July 31—After a preliminary hearing Montgomery was bound over to the Circuit Court without bail for the murder of Capt. Ryman. Montgomery conducted his own defense. He said Capt. Ryman applied a vile epithet to him in a conversation shortly before the killing, and that just before he shot Capt. Ryman made a demonstration as if to draw a pistol and that he saw the pistol. Others testified that Capt. Ryman was not armed.

Tennessean, *Sunday, August 1, 1915*

Thomas G. Ryman Jr., Shot and Killed by Wilson Montgomery

Six Bullets Fired into Nashville Man on the
Steamer *Jo Horton Fall*
Is Held Without Bail
Loss of His Position Had Engendered Ill Feeling
Between Him and His Victim

Hartsville, Tenn., July 31—(Special)—Capt. Thomas G. Ryman Jr., was shot and killed by Wilson G. Montgomery this morning about 7 o'clock as the steamer *Jo Horton Fall* was landing at Griffin's Landing some four miles below Hartsville. The steamer pulled up to Hart's Ferry where the remains of Captain Ryman were taken in charge by Undertaker Throp and hurried through town to meet an automobile from Nashville.

Sheriff Parkhurst was immediately notified and hurried to the scene and put Montgomery under arrest. A warrant was sworn out for Montgomery and the boat officials summoned to appear at the preliminary trial at the courthouse before Justice J. D. Hawkins.

According to testimony introduced at the trial, Montgomery had lost a job on the boat on account of which there had been ill feeling between him and Ryman. Yesterday Mr. Walker, the father-in-law of Montgomery, it is claimed, bought a controlling interest in the boat, on account of which, it appears, Montgomery thought he was entitled to travel gratis. He boarded the steamer at Walker's Landing at 6 o'clock in company with his wife and two lady friends for a trip up the river. As the boat whistled for Griffin's Landing Captain Ryman was at the breakfast table, but left the table to superintend the landing. As he passed the clerk, J. H. Binkley, he was informed that Montgomery was aboard the boat. Captain Ryman instructed him to register and charge Montgomery fare like other passengers, and passed on the flight of steps leading to the upper deck. Just as his foot reached the first step, it is alleged Montgomery approached him and said, "Captain," and fired three shots in quick succession, and after a short interval, he fired three more shots, the six shots taking effect. Montgomery used an automatic pistol.

Montgomery went on the stand, but said that he had nothing to say now, except that the killing was in self-defense. Attorney Russell Wright represented the boat officials and Montgomery conducted his own case and seemed to be unconcerned about the matter. He was held without bail, and is now confined in the Hartsville jail.

Captain Ryman was favorably known by many of the citizens of this section and his untimely death is deeply regretted by all.

BODY BROUGHT HERE
Examination Shows That at Least 7 Shots Took Effect

The body of Capt. Thomas G. Ryman, who was shot and instantly killed about 7 o'clock Saturday morning by William Montgomery on the steamer *Jo Horton Fall*, near Griffin's landing, was brought to Nashville at 1:30 o'clock Saturday afternoon. It was taken to the undertaking establishment of Cornelius and Martin and prepared for burial.

Upon examination at the undertakers it was found that at least seven shots had been fired, and probably eight or nine. The body bore fourteen wounds.

The body was taken from Hartsville to Gallatin in an automobile and was brought from Gallatin to this city in an ambulance. Later it was taken to the home of Captain Ryman's mother, Mrs. Betty Ryman, 514 Second Avenue, South, where the funeral will be held at 4 o'clock this afternoon. Rev. R. Linn Cave will conduct the service. The pallbearers will be Capt. W. W. Parminter, Capt. T. M. Gallagher, Capt. C. H. Armstrong, John A. Tyner, J. C. Buchanan, Capt. Joseph St. John and M. C. McCauley. The burial will be in Mt. Olivet Cemetery.

Captain Ryman began working for his father when 13 years old as a clerk on a steamer. His father was Capt. Thomas G. Ryman Sr., who started the Ryman Line about forty years ago. Capt. Ryman Jr., was made captain of the *Robt. Dunbar* in 1895. In about 1900 he married Miss Beryl Moody of Nashville. Mr. Ryman had been serving as captain of different steamers on the Cumberland, Ohio and Mississippi rivers since 1895, most of the time for the Ryman line.

Mr. Ryman was 42 years old. He had an enviable reputation as an experienced river pilot and captain. He had an absolutely clear record.

The steamer *Jo Horton Fall* is owned by the Nashville Packet Co. The boat on which the tragedy was enacted left Nashville at 5:30 o'clock Friday afternoon bound for West Point.

Wilson Montgomery, who is 20 years old, boarded the boat ten miles below Griffin's Landing, near the residence of his father-in-law, W. H. Walker, a farmer of Hunter's Point. Montgomery is married and has one child, a baby. Montgomery lived most of his life at Rome, Tenn.

SURVIVED BY WIDOW

Captain Ryman is survived by a widow and a boy, Thomas G. Ryman III, 5 years old. His wife and son were spending the summer at Larkin Springs, where Captain Ryman stopped at 10 o'clock Friday night to see his family and told them that he would stop on the return trip and spend two weeks with them. Captain Ryman had lived in Nashville all his life. His home was at 515 Third Avenue, South.

Nashville Banner, *August 2, 1915*

Funeral of Capt. T. G. Ryman Jr.

The funeral of Capt. T. G. Ryman, a prominent steamboat man, who was killed Saturday by Wilson Montgomery on the steamboat *Jo Horton Fall*, took place Sunday afternoon at 4 o'clock at the residence of his mother, Mrs. Bettie Ryman, 514 Second Avenue South. There was present a vast concourse of relatives and friends, showing the high esteem in which the deceased was held. The funeral services were conducted by the Rev. R. Linn Cave. There was an unusually large number of beautiful floral offerings, many of them being of exquisite design. The interment took place at Mt. Olivet Cemetery.

Montgomery Goes On Witness Stand

TELLS OF TROUBLE THAT LED UP TO KILLING OF
CAPTAIN RYMAN

Hartsville, Tenn., November 26—Court convened at
8 a.m. Thursday morning when the case of Wilson
Montgomery, charged with the killing of Capt. T. G.
Ryman on the steamboat *J. Horton Fall*, was taken
up. Paul Ryman was the first witness placed on the
stand. A blue print of the steamer and several photographs were introduced to show position of the parties involved in the killing. One of the
jurors was suddenly taken ill and was given medical attention by a doctor
in the presence of the judge. The prosecution closed at 9 a.m.

Montgomery was placed on the stand when the defense took charge of
the case. He testified that he had worked on the river since he was 14 years
of age and had been associated with and had worked under Capt. Ryman
off and on until the time of the tragedy. He said the first trouble between
Capt. Ryman and the defendant arose in 1908 and that after that the
former had beat him up, threatened and cursed him on several different
occasions. Defendant also testified that in 1914 he reported Capt. Ryman
for being drunk and that then Ryman wanted to quit fighting and had said
to defendant, "You make trip on the boat any time you want, please," and
that the defendant had made the trip to Celina the next day to sell some
stock. He further testified that on the return trip Capt. Ryman had asked
him if he had sold the stock and he said, "No," and that Capt. Ryman got
mad and said: "You and your father-in-law have been saying you would
get control of the line and, damn you, I will work Paul every moment."
Said Capt. Ryman knew of him having controlling interest the evening
before the tragedy. Defendant testified that he got on the boat Saturday
morning and talked with Pat Farrell; that Pat said he was afraid of trouble
and told him not to resent what the captain said. He said Brickley next

told him the captain was sore and that soon afterwards the defendant went to the office and saw Capt. Ryman at a table. He said Ryman got up upon seeing him and told Pat Farrell to register defendant and that then Ryman said, "Come here." As the clerk was getting the book he turned and followed Ryman and that Ryman turned and said, "I am going to kill you," and reached for something in his pocket. The defendant said he replied: "Captain, don't do that." and drew his gun and began shooting.

The court refused to permit any statements made by defendant after his first statement as they would not be a part of the act. On cross examination the defendant said he always carried a pistol for protection.

At 1 o'clock Thursday afternoon the wife of the defendant was placed on the witness stand. Her testimony in substance was such as to uphold the testimony of the defendant. She testified she was playing the piano at the time of the shooting, and could not hear the talking even at the table.

Mrs. Hattie Newsom, who was in company with the defendant and his wife on the boat, testified she did not witness the tragedy saying the piano prevented her hearing anything connected with it. Mrs. Carylon John, who was also in the company of the defendant and his wife, gave practically the same testimony as did Miss Newsom.

W. H. Walker, father-in-law of Montgomery, testified concerning the stock purchased for controlling the boat.

The character witnesses introduced at this time were from the surrounding country, twenty-three in number. Oliver Hix was placed on the stand and testified relative to the previous quarrel between the parties involved in the tragedy. Dr. Hager of Hartsville was present at the time of the shooting. He searched the body of Capt. Ryman, assisted by Capt. Gann. He stated that Capt. Gann pulled something out of the dead man's right-hand coat pocket. Another witness asked Capt. Gann what he took out of the pocket and he said it was not a pistol. I asked him what it was and he said it was a blackjack.

William Johnson, colored, and Ed Clyde, colored, gave no material facts. Nimrod Harrison, Mr. Armstrong, Wollie Cook, and Calhoun Belcher testified as to threats made by the deceased prior to the tragedy.

Frank Hager of Nashville, character witness for defendant, charged that Capt. Gann said that he, Frank Hager, swore to a lie, and said that because Gann cursed him in the courtroom while the court was in session. Gann was fined $10.

Murder of Thomas G. Ryman Jr.

SUMMATION OF TROUSDALE COUNTY CIRCUIT
COURT MINUTES by Jeanne Johnson

Page 611—State of Tennessee Trousdale County
Criminal Court, August Term, 1915. The Grand
Jurors for the State of Tennessee, upon this oath,
present that Wilson Montgomery, heretofore, on the
31st day of July 1915 in the county and state
aforesaid, did unlawfully and feloniously, willfully, and maliciously,
deliberately premeditatedly and of his malice aforethought assault shoot
kill and murder one Thos. G. Ryman Jr. and did so commit murder in the
first degree on the body of Thos. G. Ryman Jr. against the peace and
dignity of the state. Signed by W. R. Officer, Atty General. Murder in the
First Degree. The State of Tennessee, Indictment, Wilson Montgomery.
Paul M. Ryman, Prosecutor. Summons for state witnesses: George H.
Brickley, Paul Farrell, S. M. Stone, R. S. West, A. R. Parkhurst, J. D.
Hawkins.

Page 617—Friday, August ___, 1915. Defendant moved the Court for a
continuance, which was granted. Defendant is in custody of the sheriff.
Defendant made application for bail. Bail hearing set for hearing at
Carthage on Friday, August ___, 1915.

Pages 634 & 635—The court, after hearing all the evidence submitted is
of the opinion that the defendant is entitled to bail of ten thousand
dollars. The bail bond will require the defendant to make his personal
appearance before the Judge of the Criminal Court of Trousdale County
at the Courthouse in the town of Hartsville, Tenn. on the fourth Monday
in November 1915 and from time to time until the case is final and does
depart the court.

Order: Evidence disclosed in bail hearing: apt. John E. Gann witness for the state is in possession of a blackjack or billy made of leather and other heavy substance which is evidence in this case. Upon motion of defendant by attorneys, it is ordered by the Court that said John E. Gann deliver said weapon to the Clerk of the Circuit Court of Trousdale County on or before the first day of the November 1915 term of the Court to be used as evidence in the trial.

Page 648—Both sides announce they are ready for trial. The defendant then waived formal arraignment and plead not guilty. The Court then proceeded as the law directs to select a Jury. One was chosen and sworn in. Charge was Murder in the First Degree. There not being time on that day to further proceed with the case, court adjourned until the next morning, Thursday, November 25, 1915, at 8 o'clock. Judge J. M. Gardenhire presided over the trail.

Page 650—The jury heard a portion of the evidence, but there was not enough time to complete the trial. It was continued until the next morning.

Page 651—Jury heard evidence, but there was not enough time to complete the trial. It was continued until the next morning, Saturday, November 27, 1915.

Page 656—The jury heard all the evidence, received the written charge of the Court, and retired to consider a verdict. Court adjourned until November 29, 1915, at 8 o'clock.

Page 657—The jury after due deliberation said they cannot agree upon a verdict. The jury was discharged and a mistrial entered. The case was continued until the next term of the Court and the defendant was permitted to stand on his present bond.

Page 676—Upon motion of the defendant, the case was continued until the next term of the court.

(Editor's note: There is no doubt that Wilson Montgomery killed Tom Ryman Jr. The question the jury had to decide was whether or not he was guilty of the charge of murder in the first degree. Since the jury of the first trial could not agree, a second trial was held nine months later.)

Page 710—Wednesday morning, August 9, 1916. Both sides said they were ready for trial. Defendant waived formal arraignment and plead not guilty to the charge contained in the indictment. A jury was selected.

Page 711—Thursday morning, August 10, 1916. A portion of the evidence was heard but there not being time to complete the trial that day, it adjourned until the next morning.

Page 714—Friday morning, August 11, 1916. A portion of the evidence was heard, trail continued until next morning.

Page 715—Saturday, August 12, 1916. Jury retired to consider the verdict. After deliberation, they found the defendant not guilty as charged. It was, therefore, the judgment of the Court that the defendant go hence.

Ryman Line in Bankruptcy

DIRECTORS SAY CORPORATION IS UNABLE TO PAY ITS DEBTS

The Ryman line, a corporation operating a line of steamboats on the Cumberland River, is named in a petition in bankruptcy filed with the clerk of the Federal Court Tuesday afternoon. The petition was filed about 3 o'clock and an hour later Lee Brook, referee in bankruptcy, appointed R. Boyte Howell receiver of the company.

The Ryman line was chartered in 1894. For many years it has been operating the steamboats *Bob Dudley, Henry Harley* and *Robert Rhea* in the Upper Cumberland trade. These boats carried both freight and passengers.

The petition sets out that the corporation is unable to meet its debts, and that on August 21 at a meeting the board of directors adopted a resolution authorizing President George Doubleday to take such steps as would secure the company the benefits of the laws in regard to bankrupts. The petition states that the company is willing to surrender all property owned by it of whatever nature for the benefit of the creditors.

The company has not been making any money for some time, and in the meanwhile its indebtedness was steadily increasing. Only one of its boats has been in operation for a long time, the *Rhea*, the other two, the *Dudley* and *Harley*, having been put out of commission by the government.

The *Rhea* will be operated temporarily under the receivership until the affairs of the corporation can be straightened out.

The schedule of liabilities filed with the petition shows the following indebtedness:

Fourth & First National Bank, $8,500, endorsed by H. W. Buttorff, George Doubleday and Hunter Perry.

Fourth & First National Bank, $7,500, endorsed by Alex Perry, George Doubleday and H. W. Buttorff and Hunter Perry.

Fourth & First National Bank, $5,400, endorsed by H. W. Buttorff, Alex Perry and George Doubleday.

Fourth & First National Bank, $1,068.28, endorsed by George Doubleday and H. W. Buttorff.

A. E. Pardue, Pardue, Tenn., $8,800, endorsed by George Doubleday and H. W. Buttorff. The $800 is secured by a mortgage on the steamer *Rhea*.

Bertha Jenkins, Gallatin, Tenn., $1,600, endorsed by H. W. Buttorff, George Doubleday and Hunter Perry.

Estate of H. W. Buttorff, $3,800, mortgage on the *Rhea*.

Estate of H. W. Buttorff, $6,000, mortgage on the *Dudley*.

William Longhurst, Nashville, $1,000, mortgage on the *Rhea*.

W. B. Pullius, clerk, $106.15, lien on the *Rhea*.

Perry & Lester Coal Company, Nashville, $1,474.46, lien on the *Harley*.

Howard Ship Yards, Jeffersonville, Ind., $1,326.83.

Fourth & First National Bank, $630, endorsed by George Doubleday and H. W. Buttorff.

Nashville Machine Co., $361.

The unsecured creditors include the estate of H. W. Buttorff, notes, amounting to about $15,000; George Doubleday, $5,000; Phillips and Buttorff Manufacturing Co., $2,000; other Nashville creditors in varying small amounts about $4,000.

The schedule of assets included open accounts as shown on the ledger, $400; steamer *Rhea*, $150,000; steamer *Henry Harley*, $130,000; steamer *Bob Dudley*, $120,000; one boat shaft; $800; extra equipment, fixtures, furniture, etc., $385.50.

The steamers *Bob Dudley* and *Henry Harley* have been lying at the Nashville wharf for some time, having been refused licenses by the government owing to their condition.

The *Rhea* is now up the river on her regular trip. The office of the company is at First Avenue and Broadway. George Doubleday is the president of the company. When a reporter called there this morning Mr. Doubleday could not be seen and no one in the office was authorized to give out a statement. It is understood, however, that the concern has been embarrassed for a long time for lack of funds with which to meet its obligations and operating expenses. Receiver Howell, as the representative of the H. W. Buttorff estate, has been trying to get a settlement from the company every since Mr. Buttorff's death, but as the affairs of the concern did not improve it was thought in justice to all the creditors it would be best to ask the Federal Court to adjudge the company a bankrupt.

The company was named in honor of the late Thomas Ryman, who followed the steamboat business for many years and who was instrumental in founding the corporation. For many years the Ryman line did a flourishing business in the Upper Cumberland, especially in the matter of freight, and even now has a contract with the Nashville, Chattanooga & St. Louis railway on freight from points not touched by these roads in the upriver trade.

Mrs. Thomas G. Ryman Sr.

MRS. MARY RYMAN, SINGER'S MOTHER, DIES IN ATLANTA
HER HUSBAND BUILT RYMAN AUDITORIUM

Funeral services for Mrs. Mary Elizabeth Ryman, widow of the late Capt. T. G. Ryman and mother of Paul Ryman, concert singer, of New York, who died Friday morning in Atlanta, Ga. was conducted at the Lindsley Avenue Christian Church Saturday afternoon at 2:30 o'clock by elder James A. Allen. The body arrived over the N.C. & St. L. Railroad.

Mrs. Ryman, who was in her 79th year, was visiting at the time of her death at the home of her daughter, Mrs. Barton in Atlanta. Weakened by the infirmities of age a lingering illness which had confined her to her home for the last four years, her death came quickly. She left her home in South Nashville last June to visit Mrs. Coggins in Atlanta, as well as her other children, all of whom, with the exception of Mrs. W. E. Jackson of Nashville and Paul Ryman of New York, make their home there.

Mrs. Ryman is survived by her daughters, Mrs. Gus Coggins, Mrs. T. R. Coggins, Mrs. W. F. Barton of Atlanta, and Mrs. W. E. Jackson of Nashville, and one son Mr. Ryman of New York. Her husband, the late Capt. T. G. Ryman, builder of the Ryman Auditorium, died 20 years ago.

Acting as pallbearers were W. W. Dillard, H. T. Hill, W. H. Buchanan, David Lipscomb, R. B. C. Howell, George Allen, Humphrey Hardison and J. Bryon Hill. Burial was at Mt. Olivet Cemetery.

Mrs. Ryman was the mother of Paul Ryman, the well-known concert artist who appeared at the Ryman Auditorium last year in concert. His father, Capt. T. G. Ryman, erected the Ryman Auditorium in 1896 and it was first used as a Christian tabernacle in which Sam Jones, the celebrated evangelist was the first speaker,—Nashville, Tennessee.

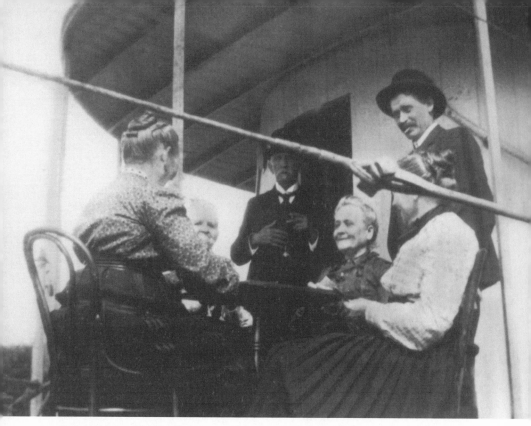

An elderly Bettie Ryman (fourth from the left) and Daisy (fifth from the left) enjoying a card game with friends onboard the J. B. Richardson.

Mrs. Ryman was born in Williamson County, Tennessee, was a daughter of Wyatt Baugh and Sarah E. Neely Baugh. She received her education at the Episcopal Church school in Franklin, Tennessee.

Mrs. Beryl R. Gregory

BERYL MOODY RYMAN GREGORY, WIFE OF
THOMAS G. RYMAN JR.

Funeral services for Mrs. Beryl Gregory, who died suddenly in St. Louis, Mo. Sunday morning at 8 o'clock following an illness of several months was held from the chapel of Dorris, Karach & Co. this morning at 11 o'clock, conducted by Elder James Allen.

Mrs. Gregory was the daughter of Dr. and Mrs. J. C. Moody of Adams, Tenn., and had attended the old Clarksville Female Academy under Mrs. E. G. Buford. She was a talented musician and a woman of much charm. She frequently visited Clarksville as the guest of her cousin, Miss Carrie Tilley, and had a host of friends there. She was a member of the Christian church.

She is survived by her mother, Mrs. James H. Moody, and her son Thomas G. Ryman III. The pallbearers were Capt. Thomas Armstrong, Capt. William T. Hunter, Ben Goad, E. F. Bean, Gordon King, William Fisk, James P. Tyner and J. H. Maddox. Interment was at Mt. Olivet Cemetery.

Nashville Tennessean, *Vol. 27, No. 147, Monday Morning, October 24, 1932, and October 25, 1932*

W. Edwin Jackson

W. Edwin Jackson, 54
Business Leader Dies in Hospital

W. Edwin Jackson, 54, lifelong resident of Nashville and for several years in the collection and adjustment business here, died at 7:35 o'clock Sunday night at a local hospital following an operation he underwent last Thursday.

Mr. Jackson, who was widely known here was born in Nashville and for many years had been in business here as the head of W. E. Jackson and Company, a mercantile collection agency with offices in the Independent Life building.

Survivors are his wife, Mrs. Georgia Ryman Jackson; two brothers John R. and George M. Jackson; four sisters, Mrs. W. Dudley Gale, Mrs. Burton H. Donnan, Mrs. R. B. C. Howell, all of Nashville, and Mrs. D. Howard Donnan of New York City.

The body is at the home of Judge R. B. C. Howell on Franklin Road.

Funeral services will be held at 11 o'clock Tuesday morning at St. Ann's Episcopal Church. The Rev. A. Donaldson Ellis will officiate. Burial will be at Mt. Olivet Cemetery. Dorris-Karech & Co. in charge.

Daisy Ryman Coggins

Monday morning, Dec. 26, 1955, in Canton, Ga., Mrs. Daisy Ryman Coggins, widow of Augustus Lee Coggins. Survived by daughter, Mrs. Jack W. Jones of Canton, Ga.; sister, Mrs. Edwin Jackson of Nashville. Remains will arrive Nashville, Wednesday morning, Dec. 28, 1955, at 6 o'clock and will be taken to Martins. Prayer services at the grave Mount Olivet Cemetery, Wednesday morning at 10 o'clock. Conducted by Elder J. M. Powell and Arthur W. Braden. Martins, 209 Louise Ave.

Paul Milton Ryman

On Friday, April 12, 1957, at 10:30 o'clock p.m. Paul M. Ryman Sr., father of Paul M. Ryman Jr., of this city, and James S. Ryman of San Mateo, California, brother of Mrs. Edwin C. Jackson of Nashville, Tennessee, age 75 years, a native of Nashville, Tennessee, and a resident of this city for 30 years.

Relatives and friends of the family are invited to view the remains at the funeral home of Joseph Laughlin Co., 4500 Magazine St., Monday, April 15, 1957, at 10 o'clock a.m. until 7 p.m. Remains will be taken via L&N train to Nashville, Tennessee for interment.

Nashville Banner, *Monday, April 15, 1957*

Saturday evening, April 13, 1957, in New Orleans, La. Paul M. Ryman. Survived by sons Paul M. Ryman Jr., Sims Ryman; sister Mrs. Edwin Jackson of Nashville. Remains will arrive Nashville Tuesday afternoon, April 16, 1957, at 12:30 o'clock and will be taken to Martin's, 209 Louise Avenue. Graveside services at Mount Olivet cemetery Tuesday afternoon at 3 o'clock. Conducted by Dr. Arthur Wayne Braden. The following will serve as pallbearers: George Donnan, Burton Donnan, Dudley Gale, James Buchanan, William Buchanan, Joseph L. Parkes III, Morton B. Howell IV, Charles Harrison, Gerald Henderson. Martin's, 209 Louise Avenue.

Nashville Banner, *Monday, March 14, 1960*

James Crozier Buchanan

Mr. James C. Buchanan, 82, of Falls Avenue, Madison, died Sunday night at a local hospital following a stroke, the after effects of a fall in mid-January.

A native of Nashville, he was the son of Edward and Jeannette Buchanan. He was married to the former Louise Ryman, who died 30 years ago.

An alumnus of Montgomery Bell Academy, Mr. Buchanan during World War I was an auditor with the United States treasury department in Paris, France. He was also associated with the former J. H. Fall Hardware Company in Nashville and with B. F. Goodrich Rubber Company in various cities in Texas. During World War II he was a paymaster with the Charleston, S.C., shipyard. His last position was with Harvey's store from which he retired ten years ago. Mr. Buchanan was a member of City Road Chapel Methodist Church.

Surviving are one daughter, Mrs. T. F. Proctor, Augusta, Georgia, and a son, James C. Buchanan Jr., Nashville; two brothers, William H. and Earl M. Buchanan, Nashville.

Funeral services will be held at 2 p.m. Tuesday at Cosmopolitan Funeral Home.

Officiating will be the Rev. E. P. Anderson, associate pastor of Belmont Methodist Church. Burial will be in Mt. Olivet Cemetery.

Nashville Banner, *Wednesday, April 25, 1962*

Georgia Ryman Jackson

Tuesday morning, April 24, 1962, at 9 o'clock at her residence 1618 16th Ave. So., Mrs. Georgia Ryman Jackson. Survived by several nieces and nephews including Mrs. Elizabeth Coggins Jones, Atlanta, Ga., Mrs. Thomas Proctor, Augusta, Ga., Mrs. Douglas Igou, Eustis, Fla., Tom Coggins, and Lee Rol Coggins, Atlanta, Ga., Tom Ryman III, St. Louis, Mo., Paul Ryman Jr. and Sims Ryman, New Orleans, La., and James Buchanan, Nashville. Remains are at Finley Dorris & Charlton, West End at Twenty-fifth Ave., where funeral services will be held Thursday morning at 10 o'clock by Dr. Wayne H. Bell. Pallbearers will be Dudley Gale, Robert Orr III, Morton B. Howell IV, George H. Donnan, Burton J. Donnan, Joseph L. Parkes III, Charles Harrison, Stephen Harrison, James Buchanan, John R. Jackson, Douglas Igou, and Thomas Proctor. Interment Mt. Olivet Cemetery. Finley Dorris & Charlton Co.

PART 7

TOM RYMAN'S
LEGACY

A Benediction

by Daisy Ryman Coggins

My father admired the "Benediction" very much. It was printed on all the letterheads concerning the Tabernacle that left his office. The name of the Union Gospel Tabernacle was not changed until after his death. He refused the honor while he lived. He wanted the religious character of the building preserved.

Benediction
by Charles Dickens

May the blessings of thy God wait upon thee and the sun of Glory shine around thy head; may the gates of plenty, honor and happiness be always open to thee and thine, so far as they will not rob thee of eternal life.

May no strife disturb thy days, nor sorrow distress thy nights, and may the pillow of peace kiss thy cheek, and pleasures of happy realities attend thy dreams; and when length of years make thee tired of earthly joys, and the curtains of death gently close round the scene of thy bed, and take care that the expiring lamp of life shall not receive one rude blast to hasten its extinction; and may the Saviour's blood have washed thee from all impurities; and thus prepared thee to enter into the land of everlasting rest.

The beautiful thoughts in this masterpiece of writing by Charles Dickens was in his heart for all mankind, beginning with his home town. The Union Gospel Tabernacle was the physical expression of that wish, the final summing up of his character. He "wrought mightily" to bring this wish to pass in various ways; he devoted his great energies to this end.

His plan for the Tabernacle included more than religious services. He founded a lecture course and numerous concerts by the best artists. He brought the Theodore Thomas orchestra to Nashville for three performances. These included choirs from the churches; they sang the choruses from the oratorios.

Captain Ryman did not object to political meetings if they sponsored reforms in city government. All benevolent projects were welcome. Old Confederate Reunions were held there. There was enough money left over from one such gathering of the old soldiers that it was voted to be used to put in a gallery which increased the seating capacity to 8,000. The acoustics of the building were perfect. Many speakers praised this feature.

William Jennings Bryan lectured there, his golden voice filling the whole building. Creatore's Band was there for three days filling the building with throngs of the music loving public. Governor Robert Taylor could always fill the building and thus make money to decrease the debt.

Captain Ryman built a "Gospel Wagon" which took the gospel to neighborhoods without churches and sometimes these services were held on Sunday afternoons in the heart of the business section. The Maxwell House Hotel steps (then on the corner of Fourth and Church Streets) was the scene of some memorable services. He had the cooperation of the leading ministers of all the churches in this work. Bishop Morrison of the Methodist Church generally conducted the services at the Maxwell House. The crowds of people were attentive and quiet. The street here was narrow and very busy, but the city gave him permission to hold a fifteen minute service, stopping streetcars and traffic in general. The Gospel Wagon was equipped with a pulpit, organ and seats for a choir of twenty.

He established a Mission next door to his office, employed a minister, and opened a night school for the steamboatmen and their families. There were nightly services there, in the church proper. It was a regularly dedicated church and night classes upstairs were conducted by competent teachers.

When Jesus was asked which is the great commandment of the law, He answered (Matthew 22:37–39), "Thou shalt love the Lord thy God with all thy heart, and with all thy soul, and with all thy mind. This is the first and great commandment. And the second is like unto it, Thou shalt love thy neighbor as thyself." Solomon wrote in Ecclesiastes 12:13: "Let us hear the conclusion of the whole matter: Fear God, and keep his commandments: for this is the whole duty of man." Captain Ryman's life is evidence that he believed and acted upon this conviction. God blessed him with success and material wealth, so that he could be a blessing to his fellowman and thus glorify God.

Appendix A

T. G. Ryman Mount Olivet Cemetery Lot

Lot #12, Section 9, 705 Square Feet
Deed No. 1306, Date Sold: 2-5-1883, Price $246.75

Copied from Cemetery Interment Card of Burials

Inft. of T. G. Ryman	February 5, 1883
Inft. of T. G. Ryman	February 21, 1885
Inft. of T. G. Ryman	July 24, 1888
Thomas G. Ryman, Age 63	December 25, 1904
Mary Elizabeth Barton	July 15, 1906
Rebecca A. Ryman	November 27, 1906
Inft. of E. Jackson	January 24, 1907
Louise Buchanan	April 2, 1912
Thomas G. Ryman Jr., Age 42	August 1, 1915
Beryl R. Gregory, Age 41	October 11, 1927
W. Edwin Jackson	October 24, 1932
Mary E. Ryman, Age 79	March 13, 1936
Miss Dasie [*sic*] Ryman Coggins	December 28,1955
Paul M. Ryman	April 16, 1957
James C. Buchanan	March 15, 1960
Georgia Ryman Jackson	April 26, 1962
James C. Buchanan	March 5, 1973

Appendix B

Inventory of Grave Markers
Taken January 15, 1998

James C. Buchanan
August 25, 1878
March 13, 1960

Louise Ryman wife of
James C. Buchanan
April 21, 1881
April 1, 1912

Thomas G. Ryman Sr.
October 12, 1841
December 23, 1904

Mary Elizabeth Baugh
wife of Thos. G. Ryman
January 3, 1847
March 12, 1926

Thomas G. Ryman Jr.
September 25, 1872
June 1, 1915

Beryl Moody wife of
Thos. G. Ryman Jr.
1875–1927

Three Infant Markers
"Baby"

James C. Buchanan
February 8, 1904
March 3, 1973

Alea Rebecca
Infant of
Paul-Lera Ryman

Daisy R. Coggins
January 13, 1870
December 26, 1955

Wm. Edwin Jackson
October 26, 1878

October 23, 1932
Georgia Ryman Jackson
February 17, 18–chipped
April 24, 19–chipped

Infant of W. E. and G. R.
Jackson
January 24, 1907

Paul Milton Ryman
June 21, 1886
April 16, 1957

Martha Elizabeth
Infant of W. F. and L. R.
Barton
March 8–July 14, 1900

Note: Some of the dates on the grave markers are incorrect.
Thomas G. Ryman Jr. died July 31, 1915.
Paul Milton Ryman died on April 12, 1957.
Georgia Ryman Jackson, b. February 17, 1879, d. April 24, 1962.

Appendix C

Ancestors

Oral tradition on the first Ryman (originally spelled Rhyneman, Reinman, or Rineman) to arrive in America says that Frederick Ryman with his wife, Susan, and two brothers came to New York from Germany. One settled in New Jersey, one in Iowa, and Frederick, who was the grandfather of Thomas G. Ryman, came South.

He had a locksmith shop in Nashville on College Street about midway between Broad and Church Street on the left side going north.

Frederick Reinman is listed as a resident of Nashville in the 1830 U.S. Census for Davidson County, Tennessee. There is an inventory and account of sale or property belonging to the Estate of Susan Rineman, recorded November 20, 1833, in *Davidson County Wills and Inventories, Vol. 10, 1832–1836, Part 1*.

Sometime after the death of Susan and before 1840, Frederick left his four sons, Charles, William, Frank, and John in Nashville and took his daughter Amelia and journeyed to California where he resided until his death. John Ryman, was the father of Thomas Green Ryman.

CHILDREN OF FREDERICK AND SUSAN RINEMAN

1. Charles H. Ryman, b. 1814, d._____
    married June 22, 1834, Nashville, TN to Prudence Reddick, b. 1818
    No children.
2. William Ryman, b. ca 1816, d. before 1872
    md. on _____ to Mary F., b. 1822, d. June 11, 1888
    Children:
    1. Charles, b. 1841, d. November 8, 1898
    2. Margaret, b. 1843 d. _____
    3. William, b. 1851, d. January 21, 1896
    4. John, b. 1853, d. _____
    5. Micajah, b. 1855, d. _____
3. **John Ryman**, b. 1819, d. January 16, 1864
    Md. April 11, 1840, Nashville, TN to **Sarah Green**
    Children:
    1. **Thomas Green**, b. October 12, 1841, d. December 23, 1904
    2. William, b. March 22, 1843, d. 1852
    3. Mary "Molly," b. October 13, 1847, d. January 30, 1926
    4. Susan Francis, b. November 2, 1848, d. February 3, 1918
    5. John C. Jr., b. March 13, 1851, d. April 15, 1933
    6. Tennessee, b. November 2, 1853, d. September 9, 1855

    7. Emma Idella, b. March 10, 1856, d. June 8, 1912

    8. Laura Adaline, b. May 29, 1859, d. July 22, 1860

4. Frank (Francis, Franklin) b. 1822, d. November 17, 1866

    Md. June 17, 1844 to Matilda (Tilda) Akin, b. 1826, d. February 14, 1902

    Children:

    1. Milton F., b. 1847, d. _____

    2. Jene or Jesse L., b. _____, d. May 21, 1858

    3. Richard, b. 1851, d. _____

    4. Walter, b. 1855, d. April 23, 1863

    5. Harriet, b. 1857, d. _____

5. Amelia

    Md. (1) Hickock in 1841 in Houston, TX, one son Ravie;

    Md. (2) Rufus Smith in CA.

JOHN RYMAN AND CHILDREN

John C. Ryman, born in 1819, died January 15, 1864

    Buried in Old City Cemetery, Nashville, but removed to

    Forest Hills Cemetery, Chattanooga, on May 10, 1892.

    Married April 11, 1840, Nashville, TN, to **Sarah Green**, born 1825, Nashville, TN, died Chattanooga, TN, November 29, 1891.

Children:

    1. **Thomas Green Ryman**, b. October 12, 1841, d. December 23, 1904 (See next chapter)

    2. William Ryman, b. March 22, 1843, drown age 8, Nashville, buried Old City Cemetery, Nashville, February 24, 1852.

    3. Molly—Mary Alice Ryman, b. October 13, 1847, d. January 30, 1925

        Md. (1) Harry Mansfield, August 12, 1862. No children.

        Md. (2) Charles Biese, about 1900. No children.

    4. Susie—Susan Francis Ryman, b. November 2, 1848, d. February 3, 1918

        Md. Francis M. Carell, March 3, 1869. No children.

    5. John Charles Ryman Jr., b. March 13, 1851, d. April 15, 1933 Never married.

    6. Tennessee Ryman, b. November 2, 1853, d. September 9, 1855

    7. Emma Idella Ryman, b. March 10, 1856, d. June 8, 1912

        Md. Virgie M. Moore. No children.

    8. Laura Adaline Ryman, b. May 29, 1859, d. July 22, 1860

PARENTS OF SARAH GREEN RYMAN
JOHN AND AMY ROBERTS GREEN

    John Green, b. ca 1794, d. 1829, buried Nashville Old City Cemetery Md. to **Amy Roberts**, b. ca 1799, d. ca 1853, Chattanooga, Tennessee.

    Oral tradition says that John and Amy Roberts Green married in North Carolina before moving to Tennessee. They had seven children. John died in Nashville in 1829, age 35, when Sarah Green (mother of Thomas Green Ryman) was four years old. Amy Roberts Green worked hard for her children. After Sarah and John Ryman were married she lived with them in her later years.

*Father of Thomas Green Ryman,
John Charles Ryman Sr. 1819–1864.*

Young Tom Ryman and his mother.

PARENTS OF MARY ELIZABETH BAUGH
WYATT WOODRUFF AND SARAH ELIZABETH BAUGH

Sarah Elizabeth Neely, b. January 26, 1827, d. November 29, 1915, Nashville, TN.
> Md. (1) Apr. 23, 1846, to Wyatt Woodruff Baugh, b. Sept. 23, 1818,
> d. Dec. 22, 1859, Franklin, TN
> Children:
> 1. Mary Elizabeth Baugh, b. January 3, 1847, Maury County, TN
> 2. Alabama Lynch (Sis Tom) Baugh, b. June 12, 1849, Franklin, TN
> 3. Zebudee (Dea) Baugh, b. March 29, 1852
> Md. (2) July 5, 1866, to John White from Ohio
> Children:
> 1. Frank Baugh White, b. August 1, 1867

John White was a Yankee soldier whom Sarah took care of when he was recovering from wounds. They fell in love and were married. John White said he could not live in the South and Sarah would not return to Ohio with him. He left Tennessee before their son, Frank Baugh White, was born.

Appendix D

Descendants

Thomas Green Ryman, b. Oct. 12, 1841, d. Dec. 23, 1904
  Married Feb. 3, 1869, Franklin, TN, to Mary Elizabeth "Bettie" Baugh, b.
  Jan. 3, 1847, d. March 12, 1926
  Children:
  1. Daisy, b. Jan. 13, 1870, d. Dec. 26, 1955. Md. Jan. 3, 1894, Augustus Lee
     "Gus" Coggins
  2. Thomas Green Jr., b. Sept. 25, 1872, d. July 31, 1915. Md. March 8, 1899,
     Beryl C. Moody
  3. Pearl, b. Aug. 11, 1875, d. Aug. 25, 1951. Md. Oct. 28, 1896, Thomas
     Raleigh Coggins
  4. Leslie, b. Feb. 19, 1877, d. Jan. 9, 1928. Md. April 28, 1903, Walter
     Franklin Barton
  5. Georgia, b. Feb. 17, 1879, d. April 24, 1962. Md. March 8, 1906, William
     Edwin Jackson
  6. Louise, b. April 21, 1881, d. April 1, 1912. Md. Feb. 12, 1901, James
     Crozier Buchanan
  7. Baby girl, stillborn Feb. 5, 1883
  8. Baby boy, stillborn Feb. 4, 1885
  9. Paul Milton, b. June 21, 1886, d. April 12, 1957. Md. Feb. 8, 1905, Lera
     Fletcher Sims
  10. Baby girl, stillborn 1888

DESCENDANTS OF DAISY RYMAN COGGINS
Daisy Ryman (Coggins) b. Jan. 13, 1870, d. Dec. 26, 1955, Atlanta, GA.
  Md. Jan. 3, 1894, Nashville, TN, to Augustus Lee "Gus" Coggins, b. Sept.
  24, 1868, Gilmer Co., GA, d. Aug. 18, 1952, Atlanta, GA
  Children:
  1. Lee Rol Coggins, b. Nov. 16, 1894, Nashville, d. _____. Never married.
  2. Mary Elizabeth Coggins, b. Jan. 1, 1899, Nashville, d. Aug. 26, 1997,
     Atlanta. Md. Feb. 16, 1924, Canton, GA, to Jack Walker Jones, b. July 4,
     1894, Canton, GA, d. May 3, 1961, Atlanta
     Children:
     2.i.   Elizabeth Ryman Jones, b. Nov. 16, 1924, Atlanta, GA. Md. 1st
            Amos Worth, (div.). No children. Md. 2nd Kenneth Langmuir (div.).
            No children.
     2.ii. Margaret Coggins Jones, b. Nov. 14, 1926, Atlanta, d. Dec. 26, 1928,
            Atlanta, GA.

132

2.iii. Nancy Foster Jones, b. Dec. 13, 1929, Atlanta, GA. Md. May 14, 1954, Atlanta, GA to Irvin Clayton, b. Feb. 7, 1926, Ft. Worth, TX. Children:

    2.iii.a. Elizabeth Ryman Clayton, b. Apr. 22, 1956, Boston, MA. Md. Nov. 22, 1991, Ft. Worth, TX to Henry Kirvin Stringer, b. Apr. 5, 1957 Children:

        2.iii.a.1. Ryman Elizabeth Springer, b. Dec. 17, 1993
        2.iii.a.2. Jack Henry Stringer, b. Feb. 6, 1996

    2.iii.b. Jack Walker Clayton, b. Oct. 25, 1958, Ft. Worth, TX. Md. June 26, 1982, Gatesville, TX to Patricia Long, b. Jan. 25, ____

    Children:

        2.iii.b.1. Sara Renee Clayton, b. Oct. 25, 1987, Houston, TX.
        2.iii.b.2. Adam Walker Clayton, b. May 20, 1991, Houston, TX

    2.iii.c. Margaret Foster Clayton, b. Nov. 23, 1960, Ft. Worth, TX. Md. Oct. 19, 1985, Ft. Worth, TX to Clinton Bradley Shouse, b. Apr. 5, 1957, Dallas, TX Children:

        2.iii.c.1. Clayton Wesley Shouse, b. Nov. 14, 1990, Dallas, TX
        2.iii.c.2. Mary Elizabeth Shouse, Nov. 12, 1993, Dallas, TX

    2.iii.d. Mary Fielding Clayton, b. Feb. 7, 1962, Ft. Worth, TX, d. July 21, 1996, Denver, CO. No children.

2.iv. Susan Reynolds Jones, b. Dec. 13, 1929, Atlanta, GA. Md. Dec. 8, 1956, Atlanta, GA to Joseph Allison Davant Jr., b. Sept. 8, 1926 (div.) Children:

    2.iv.a. Susan Milburn Davant, b. Mar. 14, 1959, Charlotte, NC. Md. William Brewer, Charlotte, NC, (div.) Children:

        2.iv.a.1. William Ernest Brewer, b. July 30, 1980

    2.iv.b. Eva Prince Davant, b. Apr. 18, 1960, Charlotte, NC

DESCENDANTS OF THOMAS GREEN RYMAN JR.

Thomas Green Ryman Jr., b. Sept. 25, 1872, Nashville, d. July 31, 1915. Md. Mar. 8, 1899, to Beryl C. Moody, b. Mar. 18, 1875, Celina, TN, d. Oct. 1927, St. Louis, MO Children:

1. Thomas Green Ryman III, b. Nov. 15, 1909, St. Louis, MO, d. Feb. 28, 1965, Baltimore, MD. Md. 1st ____ and 2nd ____ Children:

    1.i. Thomas G. Ryman IV, b. Dec. 6, 1947, Baltimore, MD.

DESCENDANTS OF PEARL RYMAN COGGINS

Pearl Ryman (Coggins), b. Aug. 11, 1875, Franklin, TN, d. Aug. 25, 1951, Canton, GA. Md. Oct. 28, 1896, to Thomas Raleigh Coggins, b. Feb. 1, 1873, Gilmer Co., GA, d. Apr. 12, 1941, Elberton, GA.

Tom Ryman's daughters. Left to right: Daisy, Pearl, Leslie, Georgia, and Dot (Louise).

Children:
1. Thomas Raleigh Coggins Jr., b. July 28, 1900, d. July 8, 1992. Md. 1st to Marie _____. No children.
   Md. 2nd Nov. 11, 1944, to Beryl Harper, b. July 15, 1922, d. May 26, 1994
   Children:
   1.i.   Thomas Rol Coggins, b. Nov. 21, 1946, Elberton, GA. Md. Jenova _____

   Children:
   1.i.a.   Eric Ephram Coggins, b. Sept. 27, 1970, d. Aug. 6, 1992
   1.i.b.   Charlotte Coggins, b. _____
   1.ii.   Bebe Coggins, b. Oct. 14, 1948, Elberton, GA
   Md. Aug. 15, 1970, Elberton, GA, to Allen Virgil Kennedy II
   Children:
   1.ii.a.   Allen Virgil Kennedy IV, b. Apr. 22, 1972
   1.ii.b.   Lori Ryman Kennedy, b. Feb. 24, 1975. Md. Oct. 18, 1997, to Harry Brent James
   1.ii.c.   Thomas Edward Kennedy, b. Mar. 1, 1980
2. Georgia Ryman Coggins, b. Sept. 6, 1904, d. May 26, 1905
3. Pearl Ryman Coggins, b. Sept. 28, 1907, Nashville, d. Dec. 1979, Eustis, FL
   Md. Sept. 2, 1931, Atlanta, GA to Douglas Rutledge Igou,

b. Nov. 6, 1902, Grand Island, FL, d. Oct. 1968, Eustis, FL
Children:
3.i.   Douglas R. Igou Jr., b. Aug. 14, 1934, Eustis, FL. Md. 1st in Aug.
       1959 to Frances Austin
       Children:
       3.i.a.   Francie Igou
       3.i.b.   Nancy Igou
       3.i.c.   Bill Igou
3.ii. Lizbeth Ryman Igou, b. Sept. 20, 1937, Eustis, FL. Md. 1st to David
       E. Price
       Children:
       3.ii.a.   Clay Price
       3.ii.b.   Mark Price

DESCENDANTS OF LESLIE RYMAN BARTON
Leslie Ryman (Barton), b. Feb. 19, 1877, TN, d. Jan. 9, 1928, Atlanta, GA
    Md. Apr. 28, 1903, Nashville, TN, to Walter Franklin Barton, b. 1871,
    Cherokee Co., GA, d. 1960, Atlanta, GA
    Children:
    1. Martha Elizabeth Barton, b. Mar. 10, 1906, d. July 14, 1906
    2. Walter Franklin Barton Jr., b. Apr. 7, 1910, Atlanta, GA, d. Sept. 1, 1978,
       Opa Locka, FL. Md. 1st____. Md. 2nd to Bessie Comer
       Children by 1st wife:
       2.i.   Walter Franklin III, Md. Betty ____, three children.
    3. Thomas Ryman Barton, b. July 27, 1911, d. Oct. 30, 1996, Jacksonville,
       FL. Md. Apr. 19, 1941, to Marie Gramigna, b. Dec. 23, 1911, d. July 21,
       1998, Jacksonville, FL
       Children:
       3.i.   Thomas Ryman Barton Jr., b. June 20, 1945. Md. May 25, 1996, to
              Cynthia Nell Copeland, b. Mar. 23, 1953

DESCENDANTS OF GEORGIA RYMAN JACKSON
Georgia Ryman (Jackson), b. Feb. 17, 1879, Nashville, d. Apr. 24, 1962,
Nashville, TN. Md. Mar. 8, 1906, Nashville, TN to William Edwin Jackson, b.
Oct. 26, 1878, d. Oct. 24, 1932
    Children:
    1. Baby girl stillborn, Jan. 28, 1907

DESCENDANTS OF "DOT" LOUISE RYMAN BUCHANAN
"Dot" Louise Ryman, b. Apr. 21, 1881, d. Apr. 1, 1912, Nashville, TN.
Md. Feb. 12, 1901, in Nashville, TN to James "JaJa" Crozier Buchanan, b. Aug.
26, 1878, d. Mar. 13, 1960, Madison, TN
    Children:
    1. Mary Louise "Bennie" Buchanan, b. June 19, 1902. Md. Sept. 20, 1926,
       Decatur, GA to Thomas Fletcher Proctor Jr., b. Aug. 17, 1902, d. Dec. 21,
       1978, Augusta, GA

Children:

1.i.   Jeanette Buchanan Proctor, b. Mar. 13, 1930. Md. 1st in 1945 to Robert Lee Hudson, b. Nov. 23, 1929, div. 1964. Md. 2nd in 1971 to James Edward Ennis, div. 1975
       Children of Jeanette and Robert Hudson:

1.i.a.   Barbara <u>Dale</u> Hudson, b. June 22, 1946. Md. 1st in 1964 to Robert Orlando Harrison, div. 1969. Md. 2nd in 1977 to Walter Gene Ward, b. Jan. 2, 1937
         Children of Dale and Robert Harrison:

1.i.a.1.   Robert <u>Dorroh</u> Harrison, b. Oct. 8, 1969. Md. 1993, <u>Hadley</u> Upchurch Dixon, b. Feb. 15, 1963
           Children:

1.i.a.1.i.   (Stepdaughter) Elizabeth Dixon, b. Feb. 9, 1982

1.i.a.1.ii.   Abby Taylor Harrison, b. Apr. 9, 1996

1.i.b.   Laura <u>Lee</u> Hudson, b. July 15, 1950. Md. 1st in 1968 Carl Watkins, div. 1972. Md. 2nd in 1973 to Luther Martin "Marty" Motes Jr., b. Dec. 3, 1952
         Children of Lee and Carl Watkins:

1.i.b.1.   <u>Carla</u> Renee Watkins, b. Jan. 28, 1969. Md. in 1993 to Timothy Earl Woodward, b. Dec.10, 1963
           Children:

1.i.b.1.i.   Timothy <u>Hudson</u> Woodward, b. Nov. 29, 1994

1.i.b.1.ii.   Brooklynne Sarah Woodward, b. Mar. 6, 1998

         Children of Lee and Marty Motes:

1.i.b.2.   Laura <u>Lynne</u> Motes, b. Nov. 14, 1973. Md. 1996, Michael Edward Toole, b. Nov. 25, 1970
           Children:

1.i.b.2.i.   Michael <u>Colton</u> Toole, b. Oct. 2, 1996

1.i.c.   Robert "Bobby" Thomas Hudson, b. July 15, 1953. Md in 1977 to Cathy Lee Parrish, b. Jan. 1, 1956
         Children:

1.i.c.1.   Kelly Melissa Hudson, b. Apr. 17, 1979

1.i.c.2.   Kyle Thomas Hudson, b. Aug. 15, 1982

1.ii.   Thomas Fletcher Proctor III, b. Dec. 19, 1939, Birmingham, AL. Md. Aug. 16, 1964, Atlanta, GA, to <u>Sheran</u> Louise Burger, b. Mar. 6, 1944, Decatur, GA
        Children:

1.ii.a.   <u>Lynda</u> Louise Proctor, b. July 23, 1966, Laredo, TX. Md. July 30, 1988, North Augusta, SC, to <u>Lewis</u> Wayne Roach, b. Oct. 19, 1957, Sweetwater, TN
          Children:

1.ii.a.1.   <u>Madeline</u> Macy Roach, b. July 26, 1996, Augusta, GA

ABOVE: *Tom Ryman's grandchildren June 1910 inside Ryman home, 514 Market Street. Left to right: Pearl Coggins, Paul Ryman Jr., James (Cub) Buchanan, Louise (Bennie) Buchanan, Tom Coggins, and Elizabeth Coggins.*

BELOW: *Tom Ryman's grandchildren June 1910 outside Ryman home, 514 Market Street. Left to right: Louise (Bennie) Buchanan, Unidentified, James (Cub) Buchanan, and Elizabeth Coggins.*

1.ii.a.2. Ryman Wayne Roach, Nov. 5, 1999, Augusta, GA
1.ii.b. Wimberly <u>Gail</u>, Proctor, b. Jan. 26, 1969, Augusta, GA
1.ii.c. Thomas <u>Fletcher</u> Proctor IV, b. June 27, 1974, Augusta, GA
2. James Culbert "Cub" Buchanan, b. Feb. 8, 1904, Nashville, d. Mar. 3, 1973, Nashville, TN. Md. July 4, 1931, Nashville, TN to Minnie Evelyn "Mimi" Stiles, b. Oct. 28, 1907, Nashville, d. Feb. 18, 1966, Nashville
Children:
2.i.   Charmaine Buchanan, b. Oct. 12, 1932, Chattanooga, TN. Md. Aug. 19, 1959, to Charles Davis Gossett, b. May 10, 1927, Jackson, TN
Children:
2.i.a.   Charles Davis Gossett Jr., b. Sept. 13, 1962, Nashville, TN
2.i.b.   Stephen Lee Gossett, b. Feb. 10, 1966, Nashville, TN
2.ii. Ryman Earl Buchanan, b. Feb. 19, 1935, Nashville, TN. Md. Feb. 18, 1957, to Ruby Jean Ford, b. Jan. 24, 1940
Children:
2.ii.a.   Deborah "Debbie" Jean Buchanan, b. Feb. 24, 1958, Nashville, TN
Md. Oct. 9, 1976, to Ronnie Michael Savage, b. Aug. 7, 1957
Children:
2.ii.a.1.   Jason Michael Savage, b. Mar. 6, 1980
2.ii.a.2.   Ashley Savage, b. Nov. 3, 1982
2.ii.b.   Cynthia "Cindy" Lynn Buchanan, b. June 16, 1959, Nashville, TN. Md. Aug. 13, 1983, to David Mowery, b. Dec. 16, 1955
2.ii.c.   Katherine "Kathy" Louise Buchanan, b. July 31, 1960, Nashville, TN. Md. Feb. 25, 1983, Ricky Gillespie, b. Mar. 21, 1958, div. 1994
Children:
2.ii.c.1.   Crystal Gillespie, b. Apr. 17, 1985

DESCENDANTS OF PAUL MILTON RYMAN
Paul Milton Ryman, b. June 21, 1886, Nashville, d. Apr. 12, 1957, New Orleans, LA. Md. Feb. 8, 1905, in Nashville, TN to Lera Fletcher Sims and later divorced.
Children:
1 Rebecca Alice Ryman, b. Apr. 5, 1906, d. Nov. 20, 1906
2. Paul M. Ryman Jr., b. Sept. 25, 1907, Nashville
3. James Sims Ryman, b. 1908, Md. _____
   Children: 3.i. Jeannette Lee Ryman

Appendix E

Timeline

1806—Nashville incorporated as a city.

1810—Population of Nashville about 1,100.

1819—Birth of John C. Ryman. Steamboats begin to ply the Cumberland River.

1824—John Ryman's wife-to-be, Sarah Green, is born.

1828—Andrew Jackson elected President of the United States.

1829—Death of Sarah Green Ryman's father, John Green (She was four years old). Population of Nashville about 6,000.

1830—Frederick Reinman in Nashville Census.

1832—Andrew Jackson reelected President of the United States.

1833—Death of Susan Rineman.

1840—April 11, marriage of John Ryman and Sarah Green.

1841—October 12, Thomas G. Ryman born.

1843—Nashville becomes Tennessee's permanent state capital.

1845—July 4, work begins on state capitol; cornerstone laid. Andrew Jackson dies at the Hermitage.

1846—January 3, Mary Elizabeth Baugh born. Mexican War declared.

1853—First suspension bridge built across the Cumberland River. October 17, Inauguration of Andrew Johnson as governor of Tennessee.

1855—State capitol completed.

1856—Tom Ryman begins fishing business with his father (age 15).

1857—November 3, Isham G. Harris inaugurated governor of Tennessee.

1860—December 20, South Carolina seceded from the Union.

1861—April 12, firing on Fort Sumter, Civil War begins. June 24, Governor Isham G. Harris proclaims Tennessee's secession from Union.

1862—February 24, Federal troops occupy Nashville. Confederate troops burn suspension bridge over Cumberland River. March 3, Andrew Johnson appointed military governor of Tennessee. April 6 & 7, Battle of Shiloh fought.

1864—John C. Ryman Sr. dies of pneumonia (Tom age 22). November 4, Governor Andrew Johnson elected vice president. November 30, Battle of Franklin. December 15 & 16, Battle of Nashville.

1865—April 5, William G. Brownlow inaugurated as governor of Tennessee. April 9, Robert E. Lee surrenders to General Grant at Appomattox. April 14, President Abraham Lincoln assassinated. April 15, Andrew

Johnson becomes President of the United States.

1866—July 19, Tennessee ratifies the Fourteenth Amendment to United States Constitution. July 24, Tennessee restored to the Union. Suspension bridge over Cumberland River rebuilt.

1867—Tom Ryman buys his first boat *Alpha* at New Orleans.

1869—February 3, Thomas Green Ryman marries Mary Elizabeth Baugh.

1885—Tom Ryman builds his house at 514 Market Street (Second Avenue, South). Tom Ryman's conversion experience at tent meeting preached by Sam Jones.

1886—Woodland Street bridge replaces old suspension bridge over Cumberland River.

1889—February 25, Union Gospel Tabernacle chartered.

1897—May 1–October 31, Tennessee Centennial Exposition held in Nashville.

1904—December 23, Tom Ryman dies.

1905—March 30, Ryman Warehouse and Elevator destroyed by fire.

1915—July 31, Tom Ryman Jr. killed in Kentucky by Wilson Montgomery. November 29, Montgomery jury cannot agree on verdict, new trial ordered.

1916—March 22, East Nashville fire. August 12, Jury finds Wilson Montgomery not guilty. August 23, Ryman Line in bankruptcy.

Editor's Notes

Chapter 2

1. Gaylord Entertainment Company, *The Ryman Remembers: Recipes & Recollections, The Ryman Auditorium* (Nashville: Favorite Recipes Press, Div. of Southwestern/Great American, 1996), 15–16, 19.

2. M. B. Morton, "Last Days of Real Steamboating on the Cumberland," *Nashville Banner,* n.d.

3. Mrs. Sam P. Jones and Walt Holcomb, *The Life and Sayings of Sam P. Jones* (Atlanta: The Franklin-Turner Co., Publishers, 1907), 152–53.

4. Ibid., 153.

5. Paul W. Treanor, "The People's Forum," *Nashville Banner,* October 11, 1948, 4.

6. Tom Ryman, interview by unidentified family member, June 28, 1892. Daisy Ryman Coggins's papers.

7. "Captain Tom Ryman's Work on the River and for Religion," *The Nashville American,* May 18, 1902.

Chapter 3

1. What was charged? Whatever fellow prisoners had of value, such as brass buttons, belt buckles, tobacco and things that could be bartered.

2. Andrew Johnson was appointed Military Governor on March 3, 1862, after Federal Troops occupied Tennessee and served until 1865.

3. Mrs. T. W. Bookhart was an in-law of Leslie Ryman Barton. Her daughter, Sarah Bookhart, married Charles Coggins Barton, the son of W. F. Barton by his first wife.

4. He was able to bribe a guard with the things he had bartered with the prisoners for bringing them water.

Chapter 5

1. General Patrick R. Cleburne died along with four other confederate generals on the battlefield.

Chapter 7

1. Mrs. Alabama (John Alexander) Rountree, also known as Sis Tom, was the sister of Mary Elizabeth Baugh.

Chapter 12

1. In a letter of May 17, 1969, Elizabeth Coggins Jones, daughter of Daisy Ryman Coggins wrote, "I lived in Nashville at my Grandmother Ryman's house many winters when I was in school." Thus these nostalgic memories.

Chapter 13

1. The Ryman house was razed in 1940.

Chapter 15

1. "Captain James S. Tyner lived to be a very old man, having died on July 4, 1935, at the age of eighty-seven years." Byrd Douglas, *Steamboating on the*

Cumberland, Tennessee Book Co.: Nashville, TN, 1961. p. 255

Chapter 16

1. M. B. Morton, Nashville Banner, n.d. Note attached to this article: "This copied by me, Elizabeth C. Jones, July 17, 1969. Mr. M. B. Morton was the author of a book, *Kentuckians Are Different*, published 1938 in Louisville, Kentucky. He died April 18, 1943 at age 83. For 39 years he was Managing Editor of the *Nashville Banner* and I think the above was published in that paper, but the name of the paper and date are not on my copies."

Chapter 20

1. See chapter 25 for a letter to the editor of *The Nashville American* from Tom Ryman's sisters refuting this statement.

Chapter 28

1. Tom Ryman was in poor health in 1901 and unable to escort his daughter "down the aisle," thus the couple's coming in together.

Chapter 29

1. This is a letter written to Daisy and Pearl by their Aunt Sis Tom Rountree.

Bibliography

Douglas, Byrd. *Steamboatin' on The Cumberland*, Tennessee Book Co., Nashville, TN, 1961.

Gaylord Entertainment Company, *The Ryman Remembers: Recipes & Recollections*, Favorite Recipes Press, Division of Southwestern/Great American, Inc., Nashville, TN, 1996.

Henderson, Jerry. "Nashville's Ryman Auditorium," *Tennessee Historical Quarterly*, Winter 1968, pp 305–328.

Jones, Mrs. Sam P., and Rev. Walt Holcomb. *The Life & Sayings of Sam P. Jones*, 2nd ed. The Franklin-Turner Co. Publishers, Atlanta, GA, 1907.

Permissions Obtained

Barton, Leslie. "Reminiscences of Mama's Childhood," "Mama's Schooling and How She Met My Father," and "Papa's First Boat." Permission of Thomas Ryman Barton Jr., Jacksonville, FL

Bookhart, Mrs. T. W. "Reminiscences of The Battle of Franklin," portions of "Reminiscences of Mama's Childhood," and recorded account of Tom Ryman's Civil War Imprisonment. Permission of Charles C. Barton, Atlanta, GA; Samuel W. Bookhart, Chadds Ford, PA; Thomas W. Bookhart, Oak Ridge, TN; William B. Bookhart Jr., Elloree, SC; Sara Louise B. DeLapp, Lexington, NC; Harry M. Hatcher III, Starke, FL; Gayle H. Weaver, Starke, FL; Avery Wood Jr., Greenville, SC; Thomas Bookhart Wood, Tupelo, MS

Coggins, Daisy Ryman. *Daisy's Book* writings. Permission of Foster Jones Clayton, Weatherford, TX; Reynolds Jones Davant, Atlanta, GA

Johnson, Jeanne. "Summation of Trousdale County Circuit Court Minutes of the Trial of Wilson Montgomery." Permission of Jeanne Johnson, Tarpon Springs, FL

Jones, Elizabeth Coggins. Portions of *Daisy's Book*. Foster Jones Clayton, Weatherford, TX; Reynolds Jones Davant, Atlanta, GA

Morris, Gail. Photographs: Statue of Tom Ryman, Ryman Auditorium Fifth Avenue entrance, historical markers of Ryman house, and steamboat detail of Ryman monument. Permission of Gail Morris, Lebanon, TN

Nashville American. "Raising Money for the Galleries," "Capt. Tom Ryman's Work on the River and for Religion," Editorial "Thomas G. Ryman," "Causes Much Grief, Commercial Bodies Take Action on Death of Capt. Ryman," "Capt. T. G. Ryman Funeral Service Is Held for Him at Tabernacle," letter to the editor "Capt. Ryman's Career," and obituary of Mrs. Louise Ryman Buchanan. Permission of Frank Sutherland, Editor, *The Tennessean*, Nashville, TN

Nashville Banner. Editorial "Capt. Thomas G. Ryman," "Capt. Ryman's Last Voyage," "Montgomery Goes on Witness Stand Tells of Trouble that Led Up to Killing of Captain Ryman," "Begin Argument in Montgomery Case," "Ryman Line in Bankruptcy," "Tyner's Reminiscences" from *Old Times on the Cumberland*, and "Last Days of Real Steamboating on the Cumberland." Wedding announcements: "Ryman—Buchanan," "Ryman—Barton," "Ryman—Sims," and "Ryman—Jackson." Obituaries: Mrs. Beryl R. Gregory, Daisy Ryman Coggins, Paul Milton Ryman, J. C. Buchanan, and Georgia Ryman Jackson. Permission of Irby Simpkins, Editor, *Nashville Banner*, Nashville, TN

Proctor, Louise Ryman Buchanan. Map drawings of Rutledge Hill and the Ryman House Lot Plan. Permission of Jeanette B. Proctor, Augusta, SC; Dr. Thomas F. Proctor III, Augusta, SC

Rountree, Alabama Baugh "Sis Tom." "A Reconstruction Wedding," and "Dot's Wedding" letter. Permission of Marguerite Louise Handley Chappell, Birmingham, AL; Dorothy Parkes Cox, Nashville, TN; Jeanne Kirtland Handley Scott, Tulsa, OK

Ryman Family Photographs. Permission of Foster Jones Clayton, Weatherford, TX; Reynolds Jones Davant, Atlanta, GA

The Tennessean. "Thomas G. Ryman Jr. Shot and Killed by Wilson Montgomery," and death notice of Edwin Jackson. Permission of Frank Sutherland, Editor, *The Tennessean.*

Tennessee State Library and Archives. Permission of Ms. Kassie Hassler, Interim Director, Public Services Section, Tennessee State Library and Archives, Nashville, TN

Tyner, Captain James S. "Tyner's Reminiscences," *Nashville Banner.* Permission of James Tyner Eves, Cedar Knolls, NJ; Patrick T. Eves, Hobesound, FL; Robert DeHart Eves III, Baldwinsville, NY; William Timothy Eves, Baldwinsville, NY; Hiram W. Ehrhard Jr., Bossier City, LA; Quillian Ehrhard, Greenwood, LA; Jean Tyner Fippinger, Orlando, FL; Barbara Mimms Tyner, Washington, DC; Jack Ward Tyner, Nashville, TN; Sarah T. Worley, Gaithersburg, MD

Index

About the Author

Charmaine B. Gossett, a native Nashvillian, is a great-granddaughter of Tom Ryman. She became interested in drawing and creative writing at an early age. She graduated from East Nashville High School in 1950 and attended Watkins Institute from 1952 through 1956 to study life drawing and oil painting. She is a charter member of the Tennessee Art League.

Gossett worked in the development office at Belmont College and later served as secretary to the executive director of the Tennessee Higher Education Commission. She studied composition and literature at Belmont, always with a vision of becoming a serious writer when she retired. A member of Two Rivers Baptist Church, she taught adult women's Sunday school classes for five years.

Gossett balances her sedate interests in genealogy and creative writing by participating in water aerobics, weight training, walking, and herb gardening. She and her husband, Charles, reside in Nashville, Tennessee. They have two sons.